RESOURCES FOR SOCIAL CHANGE:
RACE IN THE UNITED STATES

WILEY SERIES IN URBAN RESEARCH

TERRY N. CLARK, Editor

Resources for Social Change: Race in the United States
by James S. Coleman

RESOURCES FOR SOCIAL CHANGE:

Race in the United States

JAMES S. COLEMAN

Johns Hopkins University

Wiley-Interscience

A DIVISION OF JOHN WILEY & SONS, INC.

NEW YORK • LONDON • SYDNEY • TORONTO

Library of Congress Catalogue Card Number: 77-152494

ISBN 0-471-16493-3

Printed in the United States of America.

10 9 8 7 6 5 4 3 2 1

To James and Ernest

Series Preface

American cities are attracting more public attention and scholarly concern than at perhaps any other time in history. Traditional structures have been seriously questioned and sweeping changes proposed; simultaneously, efforts are being made to penetrate the fundamental processes by which cities operate. This effort calls for marshaling knowledge from a number of substantive areas. Sociologists, political scientists, economists, geographers, planners, historians, anthropologists, and others have turned to urban questions; interdisciplinary projects involving scholars and activists are groping with fundamental issues.

The Wiley Series in Urban Research has been created to encourage the publication of works bearing on urban questions. It seeks to publish studies from different fields that help to illuminate urban processes. It is addressed to scholars as well as to planners, administrators, and others concerned with a more analytical understanding of things urban.

TERRY N. CLARK

Preface

One of the recent changes in man's conception of the world is that he can alter it by force of will. This change is perhaps most apparent in medicine, where diseases which were once regarded as unalterably fatal, and were thus regarded fatalistically, are now seen as within man's control.

This changed expectation has occurred in social life as well, though with less firm results to provide its foundation. Theories of social change have begun to develop that stand in contrast to the traditional theories which were as fatalistic about the course of change in society as men once were about the course of a disease. They described social change as if it were inevitable and not under man's control, an inexorable movement from past to future.

A different orientation to social change is beginning to emerge, an orientation which sees social change as a consequence of man's action and thus potentially under his control. This orientation has led to the emergence of approaches to social change which may be termed "theories of directed social change." These theories conflict with one another because they differ sharply in the resources they take as prime movers for change. Yet taken together they do provide some increment to knowledge both in terms of the kinds of resources that are relevant to social change and the ways these resources are converted to the desired products of change.

In this book I draw together some of these emerging theories of directed change for application to a particular problem: the social, economic, and political positions of Negroes in the United States. The book makes no attempt to resolve the conflicts that arise and thus to lay out a positive program for change. It attempts to provide a social accounting framework that can show what knowledge is required and can use the required knowledge, when it becomes available, as an aid to social policy at all levels of social action.

This book grew out of a paper that was prepared for a conference on Race and the Social Sciences at the University of Michigan in October, 1967. The paper was published in a volume devoted to the conference edited by the directors of the conference, Irwin Katz and Patricia Gurin (1969). The present book is an enlargement and modification of that paper using data from a number of sources to add to the analysis.

I am grateful to a number of persons for their help. Participants in the conference described above, in particular Stanley Lieberson and Paul Puryear, were my first critics and in the numerous revisions of the manuscript the comments of Zahava Blum, S. N. Eisenstadt, Louis C. Goldberg, William Gorham, Daniel Patrick Moynihan, Mancur Olson, Martin Rein, Peter H. Rossi, and Arthur L. Stinchcombe were especially helpful. In the manuscript's many drafts I was greatly aided by the careful reading and typing of Virginia Bailey. Finally, I appreciate Terry Clark's comments and assistance in the preparation of the book for this series.

JAMES S. COLEMAN

Baltimore, Maryland
January 1971

Contents

RESOURCES FOR SOCIAL CHANGE:
RACE IN THE UNITED STATES

Introduction

The problem to which this essay is addressed is a very general one in all societies, though more acute in some than others. It is the problem of how a distinct subgroup in society, with little power and without direct resources for gaining more power, can nevertheless come to gain those resources. My use of the term "power" here is not in the sense of power over another group but a position in society having as much power over one's own life and over community and national actions as other citizens. In short, this means a position in society that makes real, rather than potential, the power of each individual implied in a document like the U.S. Constitution.

This problem may be described in such general terms because of its applicability to many societies. In many Latin American societies a large mass lives in poverty, with little effective political power, little economic strength, and little education, while a small elite controls the society. In South Africa the division is a racial one, while the large mass of colored and blacks remain without political power or economic resources. In England the line of demarcation is defined by social class and family, but still with the consequences of effective lack of resources by those on the wrong side of the line. In the United States the most important line of demarcation is a color line. Despite the fact that wide variations exist within the group of whites and blacks, it is nevertheless true that the cluster of high political power, economic well-being, education, and effective opportunity (for all these things go together) is found principally among whites, whereas a large proportion of blacks is characterized by the cluster consisting of little political power, poverty, poor education, and lack of effective opportunity.* Since the United States has long been a land of absorption

---

* I use the terms "black" and "Negro" interchangeably in this monograph, following common usage in which the two terms are both widely used to refer to the same racial group. In some tabulations the term "nonwhite" is used. This includes all non-Caucasian races, but the proportion of Negroes among nonwhites in the United States

1

of impoverished immigrants, this clustering of disadvantages in an ethnic group has been a frequent occurrence in our history. Blacks, however, were an immigrant group with three particular disadvantages. They came from tribal societies without a culture of written language. They were black in a land of whites. They were confined for generations as slaves. These three differences have combined to make the problem faced by this group in gaining constitutional power and economic opportunity a particularly difficult one.

Though I address myself wholly to this single problem, that of Negroes gaining power in American society, many of the points are of general relevance for the problem of bringing power to groups in society without it— whether it be in Brazil or Britain.

I first present a general framework within which the problem of increasing the power of Negroes can be viewed, then review research and theory relevant to this framework, and finally discuss the research necessary to make this framework useful for policy.

Any discussion of purposive social change implies some ideas, at the very start, of just what the desired or optimum state of the future is toward which change might be directed. The optimum state that I have in mind here is "equality of opportunity," broadly conceived. To specify such an optimum in any detail, however, would obviously lead to endless debate, for each of us has his own vision of the future and each will differ from the others. It is possible, however, to list those political, economic, and social resources that together constitute the individual's position in society and to take these resources as the starting point of the analysis. Those resources that are desired in themselves consist of the following set: private economic resources, public resources such as community services, political power, and freedom of action, which inheres partly in civil rights and civil liberties. These resources I define more fully in Part I; but at this point it is sufficient to list them as a set of resources that constitute the focal points in change.

The basis for social change lies in the fact that the average black in American society has lower levels of nearly all these resources than the average white. The desired change is reduction of this differential between resources held by the average white and the average black.

The framework I use involves a second set of resources as well. It consists of all those resources that have the potential for generating resources of other types, that is, as a cause of change. This second kind of resource can constitute an asset whose value lies in its conversion to resources of other

---

is high enough to interpret these tabulations as if the label were "Negro" or "black." The term "white" is ordinarily used to refer to Caucasians. When the term "non-Negro" is used, it refers to all racial groups in the population examined other than Negro.

kinds. Some resources are in both sets, for they are both desired in and of themselves, and they constitute resources that are convertible into resources of other types. In the discussion below no distinction is made between those resources that serve both as measures of relative position and potentially as convertible assets, and those resources that serve only the latter role, because it is not important to the framework itself, but only to its subsequent use. In principle, then, the framework could be used with any one or any subset of resources as the desired end products of change. These are the resources whose deficit position for a population group relative to others in society is the measure of desired change.

Economists make a distinction among goods, between consumer goods and producer goods. The first are goods that are desired in themselves and the second are used in the production of consumer goods. Consumer goods are ends in themselves and producer goods are means to those ends. Obviously some types of goods may serve both as consumer and producer goods.

The distinction I wish to make here is, in the broader arena of social life as a whole, analogous to the economist's distinction between consumer and producer goods. It is useful to think of the general framework being developed here more generally as a production system analogous to a system of economic production. Many of the arenas within which the relevant resources are produced lie quite outside the economy narrowly defined, such as the family, the school, the Congress; but altogether the system of institutions can be viewed as a system for the production of resources that men find desirable. The aim of the present essay is to begin a description of that system which will aid in the development of resources for those groups in a society that currently experience greatest deficits, in particular, Negroes in American society.

After outlining in Part I the state of the system of resources, listing the comparative deficits, as well as certain assets, I examine in Part II the question of convertibility of assets of each type into resources of another type. It is here that most of the theories of social change come to be directly relevant. These theories hypothesize certain conversion processes by which assets of one type generate resources of another type.

Such "conversion of assets" occurs in distinctly different types of action situation. As a consequence, I consider next in Part III the different contexts of action through which the conversion occurs. These action situations, or arenas of action, constitute a kind of system of production within which resources of one type are converted into resources of another. As such their results depend on particular combinations of resources and not on single resources taken alone. For example, the creation of certain assets such as economic power occurs through individual action in an occupational context, depending both on individual productivity and job opportunity. Other assets such as organized political power are created principally in a context of collective action, and depend on a combination of individual resources and laws regarding assembly. Still other assets, such as intellectual achievement, are created principally in the institutional context of the school and the home, and depend both on individual resources such as strength of motivation and the school's or home's intellectual resources.

Finally, after presenting this overall framework, within which are located various theories and hypotheses about social change, I turn in Part IV to research, asking how research results may themselves constitute resources that can help the conversion process. The research results themselves can constitute part of the system of resources for change, and it is within this framework that I propose to examine research. Thus I discuss research programs not as they will contribute to general knowledge, but as the results will constitute valuable assets for the reduction of deficits currently held by blacks.

At the outset, then, I propose to list a set of resources relevant to the general areas in which blacks, compared with other Americans, currently experience a deficit. Some of these resources are of intrinsic value, while some may be merely resources that can bring about the desired change. Some of these resources are largely absent or exist at a low level, and thus create a deficit for blacks relative to other Americans. Some are at a high level. Any of them can constitute assets through which other resources can be generated.

I have not attempted to develop an exhaustive list of resources for social change, and, indeed, I see it as premature to do so. Such a list may ultimately be deducible from a well-developed theory of directed social change. In the meantime, however, it is necessary to include those resources that can constitute important assets in bringing about change. This I have attempted to do. In a few cases sociologists whose orientation is similar to that presented here have developed classifications of resources, which may turn out to be quite useful for the purposes discussed here. To examine such a classification scheme see Clark (1968, Chapter 3).

In the succeeding sections I continue to use the terms resources, assets, liabilities, and deficits, and it is useful to say more precisely how they are employed. The term resources describes resources that are either ends in themselves or means to an end. I sometimes use the term assets when referring to resources that are means toward the production of other resources. Liabilities are negative assets, which impede the development of resources.

In addition, it is useful to refer to the *relative position* of the average black to the average white with regard to various resources, for it is this position that constitutes the focus of change. When the average black holds less of a given resource than the average white in America, I refer to it as a "resource deficit," or merely a "deficit." Thus the term deficit describes a relative position, implying a comparison to whites, whereas the general terms, resources, assets, and liabilities do not imply such a comparison.

There is one other distinction from economics that is useful to keep in mind while examining the succeeding pages. This is the distinction between "capital accounts" and "current accounts."* In any system of production certain input resources are consumed in the process, in effect constituting the raw materials for the finished product. Other input resources are not used up, though they may depreciate in the process of production. These are capital equipment, such as buildings and tools. In some accounting systems there are "current accounts" and "capital accounts," which make this distinction between the two types of resource. Similarly, in the system of resource production under consideration here there are resources used up in the production of other resources and resources that are not used up; for example, the economic resources that go into higher education are used up in the process. However, personal skills that are useful in obtaining and holding a job are not used up, but are available for other purposes as well.

I make no attempt to separate current accounts and capital accounts, and it may be that in the social system of resource production this distinction cannot be so clearly made. Nevertheless, it does distinguish two kinds of input element in a conversion or process, whether in economic activity or in other social arenas, and this distinction is likely to be important in the further development of these ideas.

As should be evident from the above discussion, I want to develop a system of social accounts that has as its central core processes of resource conversion. This essay constitutes the beginning of such a development, applied to the problem of social change in relation to the position of Negroes in the United States. Its uses should be in two directions: first, as an aid to learning how to bring about that change; and, second, as a contribution to the methods of establishing a general system of social accounts.

As the preceding discussion has indicated, this monograph has both a general and a specific purpose. The specific purpose is to provide a framework to aid both in describing and implementing the process of gaining resources or power among blacks in the United States. In its approach to this purpose the monograph will be disappointing to some. It provides no simple and straightforward prescriptions for action. It aims to raise the right questions, not to answer questions already raised, but it does go some

---

* I am indebted to Mancur Olson, Jr., for suggesting to me the relevance of the distinction between producer and consumer goods, and capital and current goods.

distance toward answering some questions, by an examination of what is known in certain areas. Thus it attempts to begin a foundation through which research can aid in bringing about a widely desired social change: an increase in the resources held by blacks in American society; that is, a reduction in the present resource deficit experienced by blacks relative to whites.

The general purpose of the monograph, which is most manifest in Part II, Part III, and the Appendix, is to introduce a new approach to theory of social change. Most theories of social change, of which several are reviewed in the monograph, express propositions about change without a systematic framework for those propositions to fit into. The present monograph attempts to provide that framework. The framework implies that social change occurs through conversion of resources—resources of one type into resources of another type. Whether the change begins through use of resources held by the social group in question, or through use of resources held by outsiders, the general point is the same. Certain resources are converted into others which themselves may be converted into others or may constitute the desired change. Conceptually, the process is similar to that of economic production: certain resources—raw material, labor, knowledge—are converted into products that are either desired consumption goods or may in turn be used as resources to produce those goods. The arenas within which this conversion takes place in economic production are factories and other business firms; in social resource conversion the arenas are the institutions of society. It is these institutions within which the "productive process" that generates social change occurs—paradoxically so because the institutions are themselves often changed and sometimes torn down as a consequence of the changes they create. This, too, is no different from economic production. The products of an industry may constitute technological developments that make that or another industry's firms and factories obsolete.

In this general purpose, then, the present monograph begins an extremely ambitious task: to lay out a general approach to directed social change which will, when completed, constitute a theory of directed social change.

PART I

Resources: *Assets, Liabilities, and Deficits*

1. FREEDOM OF SOCIAL ACTION AS A CONSEQUENCE OF SKIN COLOR

I use the phrase "freedom of social action" rather than "civil rights," "social integration," "segregation," or "discrimination" partly because these other terms have come to have special connotations in recent usage, and partly because the phrase, freedom of social action, expresses the essential attribute of which the Negro, as a Negro, has been deprived in American society. The general condition includes segregation but is not limited to it. It consists of all those constraints and strictures placed on an individual's action because his skin color categorizes him as Negro: the lack of freedom to associate with whom he wants, the unavailability of certain jobs, the impossibility of joining certain clubs or organizations or of being served at certain places of business, discrimination in housing, and the enforced payment of deference by blacks to whites in the South. Some of these deficits in freedom of action, or in civil rights, have been reduced in recent years, but many, such as normative constraints against interracial marriage, remain.

There are a number of indicators of the absence of freedom of social action for Negroes in the United States. The restrictions on such freedom differ in different arenas of life, being especially strong in housing, for example, and less strong in work.

In work, as in other areas, the evidence of discrimination must ordinarily be indirect, since the main evidence lies in residual differences in occupation or income that cannot be explained in other ways. There have been several studies that show such indirect evidence. In one Bernard Levenson shows the earnings of Negro, Puerto Rican, and white vocational high school graduates who are employed in specific trades. These comparisons

hold constant the school which the person attended and the specific voca-
tion for which he trained. Thus they do not show the lesser freedom of
action that Negroes or Puerto Ricans have in choosing among different
vocational arenas, but only that which occurs in earnings after school and
training are equated. On the other hand, they do not control performance in
school or on the job, and thus are only indirect measures of the results of
discrimination.

An example of such comparisons is shown in Table I–1 for graduates of
one high school in New York in one very specific training program.

These data show the generally higher levels of earning of whites (Other)
than Negroes and the intermediate position of Puerto Ricans. The Negro
earnings are 86% of the white earnings for this group, averaged over the
seven categories.

Another examination of sources of income differences between Negroes
and whites by O. D. Duncan used a representative sample of white males
in the experienced labor force, age 25 to 64, in 1962 from nonfarm origins
to assess the effect, for them, of various background factors or resources as
determinants of income. He then inserted levels of these resources held by
the average American Negro to obtain the income that a white would
expect to have if he held those resource levels (father's education and occupation, number of siblings, level of school attained, and status of occu-

Table I–1. Median earnings after graduation for males who worked all four
quarters of the year: graduates of High School of Fashion Industries, New York
City, 1956–1963, whose vocational training was in women's garment manufacturing[a]

Period after graduation	Negro earnings (number)	Puerto Rican earnings (number)	Other[b] earnings (number)
½ to 1½ years	2129 (30)	2278 (13)	2783 (56)
1½ to 2½ years	2468 (28)	3057 (10)	3131 (47)
2½ to 3½ years	3028 (24)	3139 (10)	3463 (40)
3½ to 4½ years	3269 (25)	3074 (7)	3728 (37)
4½ to 5½ years	3355 (24)	c	4872 (29)
5½ to 6½ years	4039 (15)	c	4284 (20)
6½ to 7½ years	5094 (5)	c	4860 (11)

   a *Source:* Bernard Levenson, Bureau of Applied Social Research, Columbia
University, unpublished data. Data are obtained by merging school records with
earnings records from Social Security Administration.

   b "Other" includes all groups other than those classified Puerto Rican or
Negro, mostly white. Puerto Ricans were so classified, regardless of race, by
ethnic origin; Negroes and Other are classifications made for non-Puerto Ricans.

   c Base is too small for estimation, to avoid disclosure of individual data (less
than five persons).

Table I–2.   Evidence of Wage Discrimination[a]

Expected income level of a white, given resources held by average Negro	$4710
Actual income level of average Negro	3280
Difference	$1430

[a] Source: Duncan (1969).

pation) held by the average Negro. The difference between this income and that actually held by the average Negro in the United States is an unexplained difference, a residual which provides indirect evidence of discrimination. This difference is shown in Table I–2.

Again, a caveat must be expressed. Some of this difference is likely to be due to resources other than wage discrimination that differed between Negroes and whites, such as the average income level in the locality in which they are employed (a higher proportion of Negroes being in the low-wage South). Nevertheless, the income differences remaining after the indicated resources have been equated is indeed large.

These tables give evidence of the absence of freedom of social action for blacks in the United States through one of its effects. They indicate that freedom of social action is not only desirable in itself but is also important in the production of other resources such as income. Nevertheless, this freedom is an important end in itself, for, quite apart from its effect on income and other resources, it serves directly as a source of well-being to those who have it.

A more direct measure of the freedom of social action held by Negroes lies in place of residence, an arena in which the constraints on freedom are particularly great for Negroes. Discrimination in residence can be seen in studies of residential segregation by race. Table I–3 shows the degree of residential segregation by race for three years in 109 large cities, separately for the South and non-South. The indices are measures of the percentage of Negroes who would have to move from a block in which they now live in order to achieve residential homogenization by race. An index of zero would indicate no racial segregation among blocks. A score of 100 would mean that each block is either all white or all Negro.

Table I–3.   Indices of residential segregation by race, 109 cities, for 1940, 1950, 1960[a]

	Total	South	Non-South
1940	85.2	84.9	85.5
1950	87.3	88.5	86.3
1960	86.1	90.7	82.8

[a] Source: Taeuber and Taeuber (1965), Table 5, p. 44.

The table shows the extremely high levels of segregation both in and outside the South for all three years. It also shows a trend toward even higher levels of segregation in southern cities. The data suggest that as patterns of deference and explicit subordination break down in the South the restrictions on freedom more completely take the form of racial segregation.

An indication of the same kind of process is shown by another analysis of segregation by Census tracts for the Cleveland metropolitan area, using data from the 1960 Census (Taeuber, 1968). Taeuber found in the national study that economic differences account for little of the residential segregation by race. For the Cleveland data he carries this further, as reported in Table I–4. The first line of the table shows the existing racial segregation in the metropolitan area. The second line shows the level of racial segregation that would exist if redistribution occurred so that only the current residential segregation by income remained. (Approximately the same result holds if finer income classifications are made.) The reduction of segregation to an index of 6% shows that only this small amount of racial segregation is explainable by income-homogeneity of residential areas. Lines 3 and 4, on the other hand, show the level of segregation of low-income Negroes from low-income whites and high-income Negroes from high-income whites. Both indices remain quite high.

Of special interest is the fact that the segregation index for high-income families is higher than that for low. It suggests that as white economic resources increase even greater discrimination is exercised by race—not by income—in residential patterns, excluding high-income Negroes even more than low-income whites exclude low-income Negroes from their residential areas. (This does not imply that high-income Negroes are more segregated from *all* whites than are low-income Negroes. Presumably, though Taeuber does not report it, the segregation of high-income Negroes from low-income whites is less than that of high-income Negroes from high-income whites.) The result is consistent with the trend toward increasing segregation in the South in its suggestion that as Negroes gain equality in other ways residential segregation is more fully used by whites. It may be that this slightly

Table I–4. Segregation of Negroes and whites in Cleveland, 1960, and hypothetical redistributions showing racial and economic components

Existing segregation index by race	90.0
Segregation index by race if redistribution occurred so that only the existing segregation by income between those below and above $10,000 remained	6.0
Existing segregation index between low-income Negroes (below $10,000) and low-income whites	77.0
Existing segregation index between high-income Negroes ($10,000 and above) and high-income whites	89.0

greater residential segregation of high-income Negroes and whites than of lower income Negroes and whites serves as an added indicator of discrimination, through the following process. When Negroes make no claim to equality with whites, when they are content to remain in a subordinate status, whites exclude them less from white activities; for example, Negroes in servant positions in the South were accorded freedom and close association with whites within this subordinate status as long as it was never challenged. A letter recently written by one old Negro man (a school superintendent) to an old white man with whom he grew up in the South, indicates how close this association was at times.

Dear Friends:

I apologize first of all for my long delay in expressing my appreciation to you for your visit to me, and my school.

Secondly, for the picture you took with me and the man whom I have considered and looked upon since childhood as a big brother. Being the only child in my family, and not knowing any brothers nor sisters, I had no one whom I could look up to nor anyone to look up to me.

Mr. James always found time to play with me, counsel me and even take me with him whenever it was possible. . . Just to be with him was enough and he was too kind to say no. . .

Our short meeting, not too long ago, did bring back fond memories. The pictures you sent to my mother and myself are treasured by both of us, and to her it also brought back her fond memories of both of our childhood days. . .

Finally, let me thank you for the influence and imprint you made on my life. If I have had any spark of success and rendered any service to my country and my fellow man, much of it had to come from the impression you made on my life as a youngster, and wanting to grow up like you.

The general point suggested by these indications of increased discrimination is that when Negroes gain resources that lead them to compete more successfully with whites, additional incentives to maintain social distance through residence arise on the part of whites. Thus in the absence of explicit and effective measures to prevent it, greater discrimination in certain areas such as residence can be expected in the future as Negroes gain resources in other areas. The general phenomenon is illustrated well by the quotas that have existed in some universities on Jews, who have been eminently successful in competing with other Americans in education.

Under the general rubric of this section I do not mean to include those strictures on freedom of social action that arise from other aspects of the condition of most Negroes; poverty, poor education, etc. These attributes bring their own consequences, some of which are identical to those described above. It is important, however, to separate out analytically those that arise from skin color itself because the elimination of Negro poverty would not directly eliminate them; conversely, the elimination of lack of freedom due to skin color will not eliminate the strictures on social action imposed by poverty.

Although this point is an elementary one, it is important to make it clear because some persons hold the simple assumption that elimination of the strictures on action directly due to skin color would somehow erase all the resource deficits of Negroes, or the equally simple assumption that elimination of differences in economic resources would somehow erase the constraints on freedom that arise from racial discrimination. It should be quite clear that neither of these simple assumptions is valid.

2. ECONOMIC POWER

The deficit in economic power held by blacks in American society can be measured in a variety of ways: by average income, relative rates of unemployment, occupational distribution, ownership of wealth, and control of economic institutions such as manufacturing firms or retail stores. Economic power constitutes both a resource desirable in itself and a source of other resources, for economic power is a versatile power, able to bring social position or political strength as well as direct satisfaction from consumption.

The average income of blacks in the United States has for some time consistently been somewhere between 50 and 60% that of whites. Table I–5 shows the ratio of the average nonwhite to white family income from 1947 through 1966, with the average white family income for those years.

This table shows the upward drift in the ratio of nonwhite to white family incomes. (Ratios of median incomes show the same slight upward drift and are about .04 lower than ratios of average incomes because the distribution of nonwhite family incomes is skewed upward slightly more than the distribution of white family incomes.) Even with this upward drift, nonwhite family income is only about two-thirds that of whites.

The implication of this difference in income levels on poverty for blacks is fairly evident. Table I–6 shows the incidence of poverty, according to the definition used by the federal government, for whites and nonwhites from 1959 to 1966. This table shows that each year a large proportion of blacks was below the poverty line. The general rise in incomes has reduced the proportions for both blacks and whites, but the proportion for blacks in 1968 was still about one-third.

Part of this difference in incomes is located in the different occupational distribution and part in the different incomes experienced by blacks and whites in the same occupation. The different occupational distributions,

Table I-5.   Average income of families with white heads and the ratio of average income of nonwhite to white families[a]

	Ratio of average nonwhite family income to white	Average white family income (current dollars)		Ratio of average nonwhite family income to white	Average white family income (current dollars)
1947	.542	3718	1957	.567	5,719
1948	.548	3842	1958	.567	5,911
1949	.527	3729	1959	.553	6,367
1950	.534	3991	1960	.586	6,676
1951	.539	4398	1961	.581	6,933
1952	.559	4722	1962	.565	7,112
1953	.587	4916	1963	.584	7,420
1954	.563	4909	1964	.618	7,732
1955	.553	5228	1965	.599	8,200
1956	.547	5619	1966	.626	8,834
			1967	.665	9,334
			1968	.681	10,002
			1969	.662	10,953

[a] *Source:* 1947–1965: Ida Merriam, "Welfare and Its Measurement," Table E, pp. 796–797, in Sheldon and Moore (1968). Data from U.S. Bureau of Census; see reference for original source publications, 1966–1969: Bureau of Census, Series P-60, No. 59 (1967) and No. 66 (1968) and unpublished data from Bureau of Census.

Table I-6.   Percentage of white and nonwhite persons in poverty[a]

	White	Nonwhite
1959	18.1	56.2
1960	17.8	55.9
1961	17.4	56.1
1962	16.4	55.8
1963	15.3	51.0
1964	14.9	49.6
1965	13.3	47.1
1966	11.3	39.8
1967	11.0	37.2
1968	10.0	33.5
1969	9.5	31.1

[a] *Source:* Current Population Reports, Series P-60, No. 71, U.S. Bureau of the Census (July 16, 1970). The poverty definition is that developed by Mollie Orshansky (1965), which in 1969 consisted of an income of $3743 for a non-farm family of four and in 1959 consisted of $2973. Data from 1966–1969 are based on a revised method for processing income data. By the method used in 1959–1965 the 1966 figures would be 12.2 and 41.7.

Table I–7.   Percentage of white and nonwhite employed males in each occupation (average over 1965)[a]

	White	Nonwhite
Higher white collar (professional, technical, managerial)	26.9	9.0
Lower white collar (clerical and sales)	13.6	7.5
Higher manual (craftsmen and foremen)	19.9	10.9
Lower manual (operatives, service workers, nonfarm labor)	32.5	62.7
Farm (managers, laborers, foremen)	7.1	9.9

[a] Source: U.S. Department of Labor (1966), Table IIB-1, p. 107.

showing blacks concentrated in low-paying occupations, are shown in Table I–7. Nonwhites are overrepresented in the lower manual and farm occupational categories, the two of the five categories that have lowest incomes.

If the occupational status of blacks was transmitted over generations, this low-status occupational distribution would serve to perpetuate blacks in low-status occupations. If, on the other hand, blacks were subject to the rates of intergenerational occupational mobility which have characterized whites, then in time—though slowly—the nonwhite occupational distribution would approximate that of whites.

This is not the case. Table I–8 shows the percentage of sons of fathers with various occupational levels, whose own occupation is white collar, for Negroes and non-Negroes. The percentage is far lower for every father's occupation for Negroes than for non-Negroes. Even among Negroes whose fathers themselves were higher white collar only 20% were themselves in white collar occupations, low or high. Thus the occupational resources held

Table I–8.   Percentage of Negro and non-Negro males in labor force in 1962 whose occupation is white collar, classified according to father's occupational level[a]

Father's occupation	Non-Negroes	Negroes
Higher white collar	69.6	20.1
Lower white collar	59.4	23.6
Higher manual	39.9	15.6
Lower manual	37.8	15.0
Farm	23.5	6.1
Not reported	36.3	8.9

[a] Source: Toward A Social Report (1969), p. 24. Data are from research originally reported by Peter M. Blau and O. D. Duncan (1967) (unpublished in original publication). Occupational classes are as in Table I–7.

in one generation are much less often transmissable into the same or higher occupational status for Negroes than for non-Negroes—in some part due to the actually lower status occupations of the Negro fathers within the general occupational class, but in part also due to the lack of supporting resources of other types to be discussed below.

3. POLITICAL POWER

As with economic power, the political power held by blacks is less than that of most other Americans. The average black is less likely to be registered to vote, and less likely to vote if registered, than other Americans. He is less likely than a white to write letters to his Congressman and until recently has known few effective ways of influencing those in government. At the state and local levels of government his political power is likely to be reduced through gerrymandered districts and underrepresentation. In addition, he is often in a minority in any political unit and thus stands the likelihood of losing on political issues in which there is a direct confrontaton of racial interests. Blacks have less experience in holding office and in the organizational skills necessary to gain and hold office. Except in those districts in which blacks constitute a majority, a black is unlikely to be nominated for political office.

Table I–9 shows two aspects of the lack of political power of blacks in the early 1960's, their minority position in political units, and their underrepresentation as registered voters. The table shows that in each of the 11 states of the South blacks were in a minority in the state as a whole in

Table I–9. Percentage of Negro voting-age persons (1960) and percentage of registered Negro voters (1964) in 11 southern states[a]

	Voting-age persons Percent Negro	Registered voters Percent Negro
Alabama	26.2%	5.7%
Arkansas	18.5	7.7
Florida	15.2	7.8
Georgia	25.4	9.9
Louisiana	28.5	9.0
Mississippi	36.0	2.4
North Carolina	21.5	9.7
South Carolina	30.6	10.5
Tennessee	15.0	6.8
Texas	11.7	5.2
Virginia	18.9	7.7
Total	20.0	7.7

[a] Source: James Q. Wilson (1965), p. 956.

1960, far from 50% of the state's adults. In each of the states the percentage of registered voters in 1964 that were Negro was considerably below the percentage of voting-age persons who were Negro. (This table understates the present Negro registration, which has increased sharply since 1964. That change is shown in Table II–3.)

Another indicator of the lack of black political power is provided by the perceptions of blacks and whites concerning representatives and administrative officials who serve them. Two studies provide such a comparison, one for administrative officials and police and the other for elected officials. Results from both studies are shown in Table I–10.

It is tempting to infer from the table that blacks believe the election system and the system of representation is more responsive than administrative structures because of the much smaller differences between blacks and whites on the election-system questions than the administrative-system questions. However, such an inference from this table is unwarranted because the two sets of questions are taken from two different surveys; they are four years apart in time and they refer to two different levels of government, local and federal. Further, political resources of blacks, as well as the subjective sense of such resources, are probably changing more rapidly than most other resources. The table does show, however, that at least with regard to administrative officials blacks felt in 1960 lower levels of political efficacy than did whites.

A more direct measure of the lesser amount of a particular form of political power held by blacks than by whites is shown by comparing the racial composition of police forces. Table I–11 shows the racial composi-

Table I–10. Expectations of Negroes and whites concerning administrative and elected officials

	Negroes	Whites
Administrative officials[a] (1960)		
Expect equal treatment in administrative office	49%	87%
Expect administrative officials to pay attention to their point of view	30	50
Expect equal treatment from police	60	88
Elected officials[b] (1964)		
Believe elections make government pay much or some attention	84	90
Believe Congressmen pay much or some attention to what people think	78	79

[a] Source: Gabriel Almond and Sidney Verba (1960).

[b] Source: Survey Research Center, University of Michigan, election survey (1964). Both tabulations are reported in *Toward A Social Report* (1969), p. 85.

Table I–11.   Percentage of nonwhites in the total population, in the police forces, and in police officers' ranks (lieutenant and above) for 26 cities[a]

	Estimated percentage of nonwhite population, 1965	Percentage of nonwhite police, 1967	Percentage of nonwhites among Lieutenants or above, 1967
Atlanta	38	10	4
Baltimore	41	7	3
Boston	11	2	0
Buffalo	18	3	1
Chicago	27	17	2
Cincinnati	28	6	4
Cleveland	34	7	0
Dayton, Ohio	26	4	0
Detroit	39	5	1
Hartford, Conn.	20	11	4
Kansas City	20	6	2
Louisville	21	6	4
Memphis	38	5	1
New Haven	19	7	0
New Orleans	41	4	1
New York	16	5	2
Newark	40	10	3
Oakland	31	4	3
Oklahoma City	15	4	3
Philadelphia	29	20	5
Phoenix	8	1	3
Pittsburgh	19	7	7
St. Louis	37	11	8
San Francisco	14	6	0
Tampa	17	3	0
Washington, D.C.	63	21	3

[a] *Source: Report of National Advisory Commission on Civil Disorders* (1968), p. 169. Police data were obtained from a 1967 survey conducted for the Commission by the International Association of Chiefs of Police, October 1967.

tion of 26 central cities and the racial composition of these cities' police forces. In all cases blacks are vastly underrepresented in these police forces, an underrepresentation that is magnified at higher ranks.

In no city does the proportion of nonwhite police approach the proportion of nonwhite in the population and in only three (Chicago, Hartford, and Philadelphia) does it exceed half the population proportion. The proportion of officers of rank of lieutenant and above who are nonwhite is even smaller, only in Pittsburgh (with 7%) reaching a third of the nonwhite population proportion and in St. Louis (with 8%), a fourth of its nonwhite population proportion.

There are, of course, recent increases in the numbers of blacks among the police and other officials in cities. Nevertheless, this rapid expansion began from a low base, for, as the police figures indicate, blacks have been very nearly absent in administrative positions of authority in America's cities and states.

Two factors provide a partial balance for the lack of individual and collective political power of American Negroes. First, most blacks are more sensitive than most whites to racial issues and even as a minority may provide the balance of power that will elect a desired candidate when the whites are split. Second, and more important, the organized direct action of black civil rights groups has come to constitute enormous power at the national and local level. Although black political power and efficacy through usual channels of democratic politics such as voting is low, collective black political power through the effective use of direct action has come to be very great.

The importance of political power is as obvious as the importance of economic power. It can greatly affect the other social and economic conditions that characterize the Negro. One evidence of this influence is the change in appeals and actions of political candidates in those districts of the South in which increased black registration has for the first time made the black vote important enough to be sought. Other evidence is the recent change in behavior of some Congressmen from the urban North, who are pushing black demands in Congress because of the newfound political strength of blacks in their constituencies. The least politically powerful blacks presently are those in the traditional situation, the rural South, where many blacks are not now and never have been registered to vote and where there is frequently no organized civil rights activity.

4.   COMMUNITY AND ETHNIC RESOURCES

A fourth resource largely missing among blacks in America is social cohesion that characterizes communities. American communities, particularly in urban areas, have a generally low level of community cohesion; but this absence of cohesion is far more pronounced in black communities. It particularly characterizes the slums of the urban North, where transiency and other conditions make community solidarity difficult to achieve. Such cohesion or solidarity would constitute a great asset, for it would give collective strength both in making external demands (e.g., on city governments or landlords) and in enforcing internal constraints (e.g., against delinquency and crime). Community solidarity would create an enormous asset as well through the creation of community institutions that would provide a variety of services and aids that could partially compensate for the absence of individual economic resources. Its relative absence leaves the individual urban Negro particularly vulnerable to organized economic and governmental forces, to individuals from outside the black community, and to the unrestrained predations of persons within it.

The lack of such community solidarity and its effects are evident in various indices of social disorganization. Table I–12 shows the rates of juvenile delinquency and venereal disease in five predominantly black neighborhoods in New York City, compared with the overall rates for the city as a whole, and the generally higher rates in these neighborhoods.

Another kind of measure shows the greater exposure to crime that Negroes are subject to by virtue of the fact that they live in disorganized black communities. They are much more likely to be victims of crime. Table 1–13 lists rates for different kinds of crime and for various income groups of Negroes and whites, all relative to the rates for high-income whites. In general Negroes of every income group show victimization rates higher than those of whites for the same income level. The effect of residential segregation is suggested by the fact that victimization rates decline less with increase in income for Negroes than for whites—indicating that additional income for Negroes does not allow escape from areas of high exposure to crime. The greater risk experienced by Negroes is further shown by the same survey, in which one out of three Negroes, compared with one out of eight whites, reported that they had recently wanted to go out but had stayed home out of fear for personal safety. Still another indication is shown by the riots of 1967 studied by the National Commission on Civil Disorders. The riots occurred in black communities and nearly all civilian deaths, injuries, and dislocations of residence were suffered by Negroes.

The malaise of black communities is shown in another way by the National Commission in a survey of 20 areas in which riots or civil disorders occurred. The survey, which asked respondents their grievances, reported the intensity of grievances in different areas as shown in Table I–14. Al-

Table I–12. Rates of juvenile delinquency (1965) and venereal disease (1964) in New York City and five predominantly Negro neighborhoods[a]

	Juvenile delinquency[b]	Venereal disease[c]
New York City	52.2	269.1
Harlem	110.8	1603.5
Bedford-Stuyvesant	115.2	771.3
Brownsville	125.3	609.9
South Bronx	84.4	308.3
East New York	98.6	207.5

[a] *Source: Report of National Commission on Civil Disorders* (1968), p. 130.
[b] Number of recorded offenses per 1000 persons age 7–20 (1965).
[c] Number of recorded cases per 100,000 persons under age 21 (1964).

Table I-13. Victimization rates per year per 100,000 population[a] for whites of $10,000 income or greater and relative victimization of other race-income groups, expressed as number of times the rate at left

	Whites				Negroes		
	$10,000+	$6–10,000	$3–6,000	$0–3,000	$6,000+	$3–6,000	$0–3,000
Forcible rape	17	0	2.7	3.4	7.1	3.5	6.5
Robbery	34	1.2	2.7	3.4	3.5	7.0	8.2
Aggravated assault	220	0.7	1.3	0.7	0.6	1.9	1.8
Burglary, larceny, auto theft	1,899	0.8	1.0	1.0	1.6	1.0	1.0

[a] Source: Toward A Social Report (1969), p. 59. Data obtained from a 1965 survey by the National Opinion Research Center for President's Commission on Law Enforcement and Administration of Justice. Data are subject to sampling error which makes precise comparisons unreliable. In particular, the "0" rate in the top row of the table is an underestimate due to sampling error.

Table I–14.   Indices of relative intensity of grievances in 20 disorder areas (1967)ᵃ

Police practices	47.5
Unemployment and underemployment	42.0
Inadequate housing	36.0
Inadequate education	21.0
Poor recreation facilities	21.0
Political structure and grievance mechanism	14.0
White attitudes	6.5
Administration of justice	4.5
Federal programs	2.5
Municipal services	2.0
Consumer and credit practices	2.0

ᵃ Source: Report of National Advisory Commission on Civil Disorders (1968), Chart II, p. 83.

though many of the grievances do not have their sources in community disorganization, they point to factors that help to bring about such disorganization.

In many underdeveloped areas that share with American Negroes a lack of political and economic power community solidarity constitutes an important asset in the struggle toward development. Examples of the solidarity of ethnic groups such as Jews and Chinese indicate the tangible assets that this solidarity provides mutual aid groups, lending arrangements, economic assistance for establishing businesses, and community disciplinary forces that reduce the costs of crime to near zero. Similar ethnic solidarity, though at a lower level, has existed among most of the nationality groups which have immigrated to urban America. The ethnic and community solidarity has had two sets of consequences: to augment individual resources, as described above; to keep individuals within the community, preventing them from participating in the larger community. Thus it may be an aid to the individual at early stages of development and a hindrance at later stages.*

The low level of cohesion in black communities has been accompanied by a low level of ethnic solidarity as well. The recent development of a black ideology, a celebration and affirmation of racial characteristics, constitutes the first elements in such solidarity. The lack of an ethnic history, carried as a cultural background and a source of aspirations by the community and the family, has compounded the lack of ethnic solidarity. The current focus on teaching black history in high schools and colleges is in

* Jewish ethnic solidarity appears to be a special case in this regard. Because of the long history of Jewish communities standing largely outside the societies of which they were a part, upward social mobility for Jews has not meant leaving the community but is compatible with remaining a part of it.

part an attempt by ethnic leaders and those followers who have begun to embrace a black ideology to build such a history.

Probably more important in the development of ethnic solidarity than the black ideology per se is the growth of community groups—some of them militant and organized as combat or confrontation groups, like the Black Panthers—in many black neighborhoods. Whatever the avowed purpose of such organizations, whether to provide organized resistance to the white community and its representatives or to run a neighborhood storefront school, the basis for community organization is being laid. This trend, if it continues to develop, constitutes a sharp contrast to the history of black communities in America.

5. FAMILY RESOURCES

Closely related to community resources, but distinct from them, are the resources that reside in the family. The Negro family pattern, in both urban and rural America, is marked by the absence of the nuclear family unit and the substitution of a matriarchal three-generation family. The weakness of the conjugal bond among Negroes has consequences for the economic stability of the family, its ability to socialize the young, and the entire set of functions that the family provides for its members in modern society.

The breakdown of the nuclear family, particularly in cities, is shown in Table I–15 by the number of black and white children whose real fathers are living at home. In metropolitan areas (for Negroes, principally central cities) only slightly more than half the Negro children at this age level are living in an intact family.

One effect on the families of the next generation is shown by the levels

Table I–15. **Percentage of students in the ninth grade of American public schools whose real fathers are living at home (1965)**[a]

	Negro	White
In metropolitan areas	54.0%	84.3%
Outside metropolitan areas	59.8	83.0

[a] *Source:* Special tabulations from survey of *Equality of Educational Opportunity* (1966), carried out by the U.S. Office of Education. There is also a small proportion of children in each race for whom there is a stepfather present (although some stepfathers were probably misreported as real fathers). A special tabulation recently carried out by the Census Bureau for the White House gives estimates very close to these for 6-13-year-olds and 14-17-year-olds for 1968, though not separated by metropolitan versus nonmetropolitan. These estimates are 90 and 86% for whites and 59 and 58% for Negroes (Moynihan, personal communication, June 17, 1969).

Table I-16. Percentage of nonwhite births that are illegitimate in selected years[a]

1940	16.8
1950	18.0
1960	21.6
1966	26.3
1967	29.4
1968	31.2

[a] *Source:* 1940–1966: *Report of National Advisory Commission on Civil Disorders* (1968), p. 130, 1967, 1968: U.S. Department of Health, Education, and Welfare (1970a,b).

of illegitimacy. Table I-16 shows the increase in illegitimacy from 1940 to 1968.

These levels of illegitimacy are an indication of the proportion of Negro families that are broken before they start, families that never had a husband-wife structure. Obviously, in the absence of some opportunities for escape the individuals born into such a pattern perpetuate it into the next generation.

6. PERSONAL RESOURCES

The average black in America suffers serious deficits of personal resources relative to other Americans, resources that could generate many other resources. He has a relatively low level of academic achievement in school, which prevents further education and narrows the range of available jobs, a lack of organizational skills, a lack of information that could make rational action possible, and an absence of the feeling that he can affect his own situation. The absence of these resources helps produce other personal liabilities: mental illness, crime, and such self-destructive actions as delinquency and addiction to drugs and alcohol. The deficits of personal resources are partly due to the absence of resources of the types described in earlier sections, but in turn, they help perpetuate those deficits; for example, the low level of personal resources in one generation of females makes it impossible for that generation of females to compensate for the absence of family cohesion in socializing the next generation. The lack of personal resources in males makes it impossible for them to take full advantage of greater freedom of access to jobs, as patterns of discrimination are reduced.

One of the personal resources that differ for blacks and whites is the level of schooling attained. There has been, and continues to be, a consistent difference in the number of years of school attended. One measure of this

Table I–17.   Percentage completing grade 12 for cohorts aged 16–20 in indicated years[a]

	Males		Females	
	White	Nonwhite	White	Nonwhite
1920	27.8	9.8	32.7	11.5
1925	34.7	12.4	39.5	14.8
1930	41.4	15.5	45.1	17.7
1935	49.9	21.4	52.8	23.2
1940	55.8	26.7	59.8	30.3
1945	56.2	29.8	61.1	35.2
1950	69.3	43.8	68.1	41.8
1955	72.7	53.4	72.8	51.3

[a] Source: Tabulation from B. Duncan, "Trends in Output and Distribution of Schooling," in Sheldon and Moore (1968), Table 26, p. 655. Original source for first six cohorts: U.S. Census of Population (1960) v. 1, part 1, Table 173. For last two cohorts, Current Population Reports, Series P-20, No. 158 (December 1966), Table 4. Because of different survey procedures, proportions may be overstated in the last two cohorts in relation to the first six.

difference is the proportion of persons of given ages who have completed high school. This is shown in Table I–17. Evidence on cohorts younger than those shown in the table (but for whom the proportion completing grade 12 has not yet reached its final level) indicates that the gap has reduced in recent years. Yet the gap continues at higher levels in the proportion continuing beyond high school.

Even when educational attainment in years of school completed is the same, the level of skills attained through this schooling differs for blacks and whites—in part because of the different school resources to which blacks and whites are exposed but even more because of the different family and community resources that support or constrain the child's achievement in school.

The deficit in basic skills of verbal and mathematical achievement, even for those Negroes who have reached the 12th grade in school, is shown in Table I–18, which gives the number of grade levels that the average Negro in the North and South is behind the average white in the urban North at three points in school: grades 6, 9, and 12.*

This deficit has direct consequences for those avenues of further activity

* These increasing gaps in terms of years behind do not mean in all cases that the distribution of Negroes falls farther below the distribution of whites with increasing years. Northern urban Negroes are about one standard deviation below northern urban whites at grades 1, 3, 6, 9, and 12. Southern rural Negroes, the lowest group, are the same distance below at grade 1 (one standard deviation), but fall to 1.9 standard deviations below northern urban whites at grade 12, meaning that only about 5% are above the average of northern urban whites.

Table I–18.   Number of grade levels average Negro in North and South is behind average northern urban white at beginning of grades 6, 9, 12[a]

| | Verbal achievement | | | | Math achievement | | | |
| | North | | South | | North | | South | |
	Urban	Non-urban	Urban	Non-urban	Urban	Non-urban	Urban	Non-urban
Grade 6	1.7	1.9	2.0	2.4	2.1	2.2	2.4	2.6
9	2.4	2.7	3.0	3.8	2.8	2.8	3.1	3.6
12	3.4	4.2	4.2	5.1	5.1	5.2	5.6	6.1

[a] *Source: Equality of Educational Opportunity* (1966). Calculated from tabulations on pp. 274–275.

that use as entrance criteria levels of achievement in these two basic skills. Further education is most prominent among them, but many jobs without formal educational requirements do require passing some criterion level of reading comprehension and numerical facility. Military service uses the Armed Forces Qualifying Test, which measures these same skills, as a selection criterion. Those who fail to achieve a minimal score on this test are disqualified from entrance into the armed forces.

In general those who score below the tenth percentile in AFQT class V have been rejected, though depending on the military needs for manpower, an additional number of men from the next higher level, class IV, have been rejected through an additional test, the AQB (Army Qualification Battery). The proportion of Negro and non-Negro draftees rejected at the preinduction examination because of failing these tests is shown in Table I–19. Because of increasing military manpower needs, mental requirements differ at various times; but even at the lowest point (1967) 31.1% of Negroes were rejected because of failure to pass the tests.

An additional tabulation, showing the rejection rates for 1967 by state, is given in Table I–20, with states ordered by increasing percentages of non-Negro failures. This table shows that in general as the rejection rates for non-Negroes go up, the rates for Negroes do as well, showing wide

Table I–19.   Percentage of draftees disqualified because of low scores on AFQT and supplementary achievement tests[a]

	Negroes	Non-Negroes
July 1950 through December 1963	52.1	12.8
1964	68.3	20.6
1965	59.6	14.7
1966	43.4	8.7
1967	31.1	8.7

[a] *Source:* Karpinos (1968), Table 10, p. 25. See p. 21 for changes in standards from 1951 through 1967.

Table I–20. Percentage of draftees in each state disqualified because of low scores on AFQT and supplementary achievement tests, 1967. States ordered by percent of non-Negroes failing[a]

	Non-Negro	Negro
Minnesota	2.3	22.8
Utah	2.3	...
Washington	2.4	17.8
Michigan	2.5	18.7
South Dakota	2.8	...
New Hampshire	2.9	...
Montana	3.1	...
Nebraska	3.1	18.2
Pennsylvania	3.1	27.0
Iowa	3.2	...
Kansas	3.2	18.4
Wisconsin	3.3	36.6
Oregon	3.4	7.6
Rhode Island	3.4	8.2
North Dakota	3.6	...
Nevada	4.0	37.8
Vermont	4.1	...
Louisiana	4.3	33.9
Maine	4.6	...
District of Columbia	4.7	23.6
Idaho	4.7	28.6
Oklahoma	4.8	25.6
Florida	4.9	28.8
Wyoming	4.9	...
Indiana	5.2	24.1
Delaware	5.4	34.7
Ohio	5.8	24.7
Colorado	5.9	18.3
Georgia	6.1	37.3
California	6.3	16.1
Missouri	6.3	28.1
Massachusetts	6.7	24.0
Maryland	7.1	23.9
New Mexico	7.1	18.6
Illinois	7.2	32.9
South Carolina	7.4	44.8
Texas	7.4	26.1
Mississippi	7.6	52.8
Alaska	8.0	...
New Jersey	8.6	40.5
Alabama	9.4	45.0
Tennessee	9.6	29.6
Virginia	9.6	33.0
Arizona	9.7	27.5
Arkansas	10.7	38.5

Table I–20 continued

	Non-Negro	Negro
New York	12.0	19.0
Hawaii	12.1	. . .
West Virginia	12.2	28.4
Connecticut	13.0	34.8
Kentucky	13.0	29.9
North Carolina	13.1	45.1
Guam	30.6	. . .
Puerto Rico	45.0	61.2

ᵃ *Source:* Karpinos (1968), Tables 17, 18, pp. 40–43.

variation between the general levels of culture and literacy among the states. In two states, Oregon and Rhode Island, the rejection rates for Negroes are lower than those for non-Negroes in 13 states; and in Puerto Rico the rejection rates for non-Negroes (using a Spanish language test) is higher than the Negro rate in all but two states. Nevertheless the table shows the much lower level of general academic resources of Negroes at the end of public education, and the effect of this in providing barriers to subsequent roles, in this case military service.

Besides these personal resources which are measures of academic achievement or school attainment, there are other important personal resources for which the average Negro stands in a deficit position relative to whites. One of these is an individual's sense of control of his environment, his belief that he can control his future through his own actions. Table I–21

Table I–21. Percentage of 12th grade Negroes and whites in North and South who agree, are not sure, and disagree that "Good luck is more important than hard work for success"ᵃ

	Negroes				Whites			
	North		South		North		South	
	Urban	Non-urban	Urban	Non-urban	Urban	Non-urban	Urban	Non-urban
Agree (good luck)	10	15	12	17	4	4	4	4
Not sure	13	18	13	17	7	6	5	5
Disagree (hard work)	77	67	75	66	89	90	91	91

ᵃ *Source:* Equality of Educational Opportunity (1966), calculated from Table 3.13.14, p. 289. Subregions were averaged weighted by population. Proportions are based on those who responded. Some students did not finish the questionnaire and, especially among Negroes in the South, nonresponse rates were high, reaching 20% in one region. Since these students would likely have had a higher rate of "good luck" response, the Negro-white differences are probably understated in relation to the population of 12th graders. Additional understatement probably arises from the greater nonenrollment rate of Negroes at 12th-grade level.

reports the responses of Negroes and whites in the North and South to a question that elicits this belief.

The importance of attitudes such as this is the effect such an orientation toward the environment can have on other resources, by creating an active, driving stance toward the environment rather than a passive one. Suggestive evidence of its importance is provided by a striking result: those 9th-grade Negroes who gave the "hard work" response scored higher on the verbal achievement test, both in the North and South, than those whites who gave the "good luck" response, even though as Table I–17 showed, the average Negro scored from 2.7 to 3.8 years (in different regions) behind northern urban whites and nearly as far behind whites from other regions. Although it is not possible to separate cause and effect by use of these data, this result does suggest an enormous potential impact of such an orientation in the creation of other resources.

Another general area of personal resources is health. From birth Negroes experience poorer health, greater chance of disease, sickness, and death than whites. Table I–22 compares the life expectancy of whites and Negroes at particular ages. Although these "expectancies" are based on cohorts whose lives are already past and cannot be considered true expectancies for persons currently of the indicated ages, comparisons between Negroes and whites at a given age level may be made. In every case, except for the oldest age (75), Negro life expectancy is lower.

The largest difference in death rates for Negroes and whites is in infancy. Infant mortality (deaths before one year) is almost twice as high for Negroes as whites, and as Table I–23 shows the ratio is higher in the period between one month and one year.

Indicators of health also may be found in the disability it creates, keeping

Table I–22. Life expectancies expressed as number of years remaining at selected age, calculated for 1964[a]

	Males		Females	
	White	Nonwhite	White	Nonwhite
0	67.7	61.1	74.6	67.2
5	64.6	59.5	71.3	65.1
15	54.9	49.9	61.5	55.4
25	45.6	40.9	51.8	45.9
45	27.4	24.7	32.9	28.7
65	13.0	12.8	16.3	15.6
75	8.1	9.8	9.6	11.1

[a] Source: Toward A Social Report (1969), p. 6. See text for caution in interpreting table.

Table I-23.   Infant mortality, per 1000 live births, for whites and nonwhites, 1940-1965[a]

	Neonatal (0-28 days old)		Postneonatal (28 days to one year)	
	White	Nonwhite	White	Nonwhite
1940	27.2	39.7	16.0	34.1
1950	19.4	27.5	7.4	17.0
1960	17.2	26.9	5.7	16.4
1965	16.1	25.4	5.4	14.9

[a] *Source: Report of the National Advisory Commission on Civil Disorders* (1968), p. 136. More detailed data (year by year from 1935-1965 in chart form) are presented for all infant mortality for whites and nonwhites by Iwao M. Moriyama, "Problems in The Measurement of Health Status," in Sheldon and Moore (1968), p. 574.

people out of work and dependent on another for care. Here also the health resources of Negroes are fewer than those of whites, and show higher levels of disability (defined to include number of days of restricted activity, bed disability, and days lost from work). Table I-24 shows that for every age group except 17-24 the rates of disability of males in the labor force is higher for nonwhites than whites.

This description of deficits in personal resources of the average Negro in relation to the average white does not imply that the average Negro has fewer of *all* types of personal resources than the average white. It does imply, however, that the balance of personal resources is such that even if all other resources, including political power, economic power, and freedom of action, were equal at a given point in life, the average Negro in America could not maintain these resources at the same level as the average non-Negro.

Table I-24.   Average number of disability days per year for white and nonwhite males in the labor force, by age, July 1961-June 1963[a]

	Males 17 and older	
	White	Nonwhite
Total	20.5	25.3
17-24	12.6	10.2
25-44	16.6	22.7
45-64	26.2	35.9
65 +	37.9	42.9

[a] *Source:* U.S. Department of Labor (1966), Table IV D-12, p. 229. Data obtained by the Health Interview Survey of the Public Health Service.

7. ATTRIBUTES OF THE LARGER SOCIETY THAT CONSTITUTE LIABILITIES

a. White Prejudice

An important liability for Negroes is the prejudice of many whites that leads them to act differently to Negroes than to other whites. This prejudice, both as it is directly acted on, and as it constitutes an expectation which even whites with little prejudice will use as a basis of action (e.g., when because of fear of large economic loss they are caught up in panic selling of houses when Negroes move into a neighborhood), is the principal source of the first listed deficit, lack of freedom in social action. The elimination of anti-Negro prejudice would have an important effect in increasing other resources held by Negroes. This is not to say that the most efficient way to generate certain of those resources is to eliminate prejudice, for prejudice may change only in response to increases in other resources, such as economic and political resources. Also, many of the resource deficits have causes other than white prejudice, even those that appear most directly derivative from such prejudice. A juxtaposition of two sets of data, residential segregation from 1940 to 1960 (from Table I–3) and white attitudes toward residential integration from 1942 to 1963, shows this well (Table I–25). The data indicate that when social and economic factors are combined with attitudinal prejudice the resulting social configuration is not a simple reflection of the level of prejudice but is much more complex.

b. Occupational Structure

A second important attribute of the larger society that constitutes a liability for Negroes is the present state of the occupational structure. This structure now, more than at any time in the past and more than that of any other nation, has a paucity of unskilled and semiskilled jobs requiring little education. Such jobs have been the first after immigration for many groups. They offer an entry into the employed labor force and are often a training ground for other occupations. For many persons they have been the first rung on the ladder of economic independence. Now that rung is less often available than in the past.

c. Division of Labor

A third characteristic of American society that constitutes a liability for many Negroes, and for lower-class persons generally, is that the economy

Table I-25.   Indices of residential segregation by race, 109 cities, for 1940, 1950, 1960, and percentage of whites who approve residential integration in 1942, 1956, June and December 1963, 1965, and 1968[a]

	South		North	
	Residential segregation	Percentage of whites approving residential integration	Residential segregation	Percentage of whites approving residential integration
1940	84.9		85.5	
1942		12		42
1950	88.5		86.3	
1956		38		58
1960	90.7		82.8	
1963 June		44		68
1963 December		51		70
1965		58		81
1968		57		83

[a] *Source:* For residential segregation see Table I-3. For attitudes toward residential integration the question asked was, "If a Negro with the same income and education as yours moved into your block, would it make any difference to you?" Data on 1942, 1956, 1963 from Paul B. Sheatsley (1966, Table 1, p. 222). Data on 1965, 1968 by personal communication from Paul B. Sheatsley (July 1, 1969) unpublished data from NORC surveys of October 1965 and April 1968.

is far from a subsistence one, and has a very high level of division of labor. This means that many necessities of life, which in a subsistence economy can be provided by the individual's own labor, must be purchased with money. For a simple example, in some societies working-class families are able to keep chickens in the back yard and to raise a few vegetables. In the rural areas from which urban Negroes have migrated this pattern is even more frequent, but in the parts of the urban North to which Negroes have migrated such partial direct subsistence by one's own labor is not possible. The necessities must be obtained indirectly, through work at a job for which money is paid.

The nonsubsistence character of the American economy increases sharply the impact of those conditions (such as slowdowns in the economy or lack of personal resources necessary to hold a job) that lead to unemployment. The importance of money for subsistence living acts as a multiplier of the impact of certain economic conditions and personal resources on resources in other areas.

There are many more attributes of the society that constitute liabilities for Negroes, but without adequate theoretical framework for relating them to other elements it is not useful to list them. The three attributes listed above give some idea of the range they cover. Although no list of such attributes is given, some are mentioned at later points when appropriate.

The list of types of resources, and discussion of their differing levels for blacks and whites, indicates the areas in which social change is necessary for blacks to have levels of resources comparable to those of whites. The resource deficits range all the way from conditions existing in the white community or in institutions controlled by whites to the personal character- istics of blacks and the absence of a cultural history. Some of the resources listed are important as being desirable in themselves. All are important through their effects in increasing or reducing other resources. The question then becomes one of how existing deficits of blacks in relation to other Americans are to be overcome. What resources or assets can be used to generate resources of another type; and, in turn, how will that change pro- vide assets that eliminate certain other deficits described above? The problem appears enormous, but it should be placed in some perspective. There are at present certain assets that did not exist a few years ago. Some of these assets are described below.

8. POLITICAL ASSETS

In at least four ways there have been recent sharp increases in the polit- ical power of Negroes. First, their migration into the urban North gave them political strength in the Congress through congressmen whose political interests came to be dependent on black interests. Second, there has been an increase in personal resources on the part of some young blacks in both South and North due to urbanization and education. Third, the northern migration has led to an increasing focus of attention on the condition of blacks in America by whites, particularly younger whites with high organi- zational and political skill and the lack of opportunity to use them. This sympathetic attention itself constitutes a resource that was absent only a few years earlier. These last two changes led to the civil rights movement and the enormous political power that movement has created. This in turn has decreased the deficit in black freedom of action (through protest move- ments at the local level and legislation at all levels) and the deficit in political power (through voter registration drives in the South) and has created personal resources by giving black activists organizational skill and a belief in their ability to affect their situation. At present there are political assets that offer a potential resource for conversion into resources directly held by the average Negro which did not exist some years ago.

One final political asset has increased even more recently than those mentioned above. This is the capability for organized violence and the threat of such violence. Organized violence is the ultimate political weapon and must be regarded as a political tool. It is, of course, a dangerous one to use because it invites a violent response. However, to use the riots as an example, it would be naïve to assume that along with the economic liabilities brought by the riots there were not assets as well in the form of increased resources devoted to ghetto problems, increased credit for Negro merchants, and increased attention to unemployment in the ghetto.* Apart from the riots, there have come into being in a number of cities organized groups—some of them, like the Blackstone Rangers in Chicago, quite explicitly gangs—engaged in both legal and illegal activities, who sometimes challenge the activities of the police, and whose very presence changes the balance of power in the community. It may be noted that if these groups move in legitimate directions they may constitute the basis of a higher level of community cohesion than black urban neighborhoods have ever known.

9. EXPANDING WEALTH OF THE NATION

An important asset currently held by Negroes in America is the rapid expansion of wealth in the society. At first glance it appears that this asset is valuable principally in increasing public expenditures on education, housing, family support, health, and other areas that can create certain resources and facilitate the growth of others.

However, to look at the question in this way is to take too narrow a view, for the rate of expansion of the country's wealth has indirect consequences as well. An example is the passage of the Civil Rights Act of 1964. This bill required no allocation of the country's wealth. It was not a public welfare measure but merely a redistribution of political resources. Yet one action that made this bill possible was the passage of an act to aid cotton-growing states. This act, influenced by expanding economic resources, reduced the opposition of Southern legislators to the Civil Rights Act to a level that made its passage possible.

The general principle of which this is an example is that at a time of expanding resources conflict in which one side must lose can be readily transformed into action in which both sides gain. If resources are expanding, action is possible to make both sides better off than they were before. If resources are stable or contracting, no such action can be taken. It is im-

---

* There have clearly been both direct economic liabilities and benefits to ghettoes in which riots have occurred. The liabilities have been in higher prices due to increased costs to merchants of doing business (insurance costs, repair of property, private guards) and to the flight of merchants from ghetto areas. The benefits have been those described in the text. The net economic benefit or loss experienced by the average ghetto resident has not been determined by research so far as I am aware.

portant to note that the crucial variable that allows action is not the absolute size of the economic resources but their rate of expansion.

The behavioral fact on which his principle depends is that people will fight harder against the loss of what they have than for some new gain. When resources are expanding, there can always be some compensation that will make all groups at least as well off as they were before, and some better off. Such an allocation will be much less strongly resisted in a legislature or other political body than any redistribution in which some groups will lose.*

This principle has special relevance of the problem of reducing Negro deficits, for if the set of resources in the nation were fixed, no matter at how high a level of economic wealth, an increase in black resources could come only through reduction of the assets held by whites. Since it is not fixed, actions can be taken to increase black resources without reducing those of whites. In short, it means that actions can be taken that would otherwise confront immovable opposition.

An excellent example of this principle within the economy is the reduction of job discrimination in expanding occupations versus stable or contracting ones. In expanding occupations the effects of discrimination can be rapidly reduced by recruitment of Negroes to new jobs. In stable occupations, however, such as many crafts, to produce the same effect means to replace current white jobholders with blacks, an action in which gain for a specific black is accompanied by loss for a specific white. It is not surprising, then, that racial integration has proceeded more quickly in expanding occupations than in stable or contracting ones.

Another example of this principle is found in school integration in northern cities. Demands for such integration have been quite powerful. Yet in their period of greatest power they were not powerful enough to bring about integration in the face of opposition by whites. It is likely that whatever measures were instituted, at a local, state, or national level, to bring about integration, white parents would find a way around them (e.g., middle-class parents can now afford private schools) if they felt that their children were being hurt by integration. Since there is evidence that a child's achievement is affected by the socioeconomic level of his fellow students and since many white parents are racially prejudiced, they are likely to feel that their children are being hurt by integration.

A viable solution would appear to be to accompany school integration with an improvement in the quality of the schools which would compensate whites for the reduction in school quality that occurred with the in-

* For a discussion of expansion and contraction of economic and other resources see Parsons (1963) and Coleman (1963).

troduction of large numbers of lower-class children. That is, the fact of integration acts to increase resources available to Negro children. In order for this to be possible it must be done without greatly reducing assets of the white children necessary to it. In a system of expanding economic resources this is possible simply by allocating some portion of this increment in wealth to the creation of schools that are both integrated and improved.

There is another principle that is closely related to the indirect benefits that expanding wealth can provide. This is the fact that *even* when no actions can be taken that will benefit all it is sometimes possible that all may gain in the end. The conditions for such general gain are expressed in the "compensation principle" in economics, first stated by Kaldor (1939), by using the repeal of the Corn Laws (a tax on import of grain) in England as an example. If there is a change in an economic system (e.g., repeal of the Corn Laws) so that those who gain (e.g., consumers) can compensate those who lose (e.g., farmers) in such a way that both are better off, the change is one that benefits the system as a whole, since all can be better off than before. A move in which all are at least as well off, and some are better off, is described in economics as a Pareto-optimal move. What is often problematic, however, is how to create a Pareto-optimal move when the concrete action to be taken (e.g., repeal of Corn Laws) benefits some and hurts others. A frequent way is that described above in the Civil Rights Act example: to package together, either in the same bill or in agreements to pass two bills, actions that will "compensate" those who stand to lose if the single action alone were passed.

Even so, it is often difficult to devise a joint action that will include the compensation; for example, economists have shown that racial discrimination brings a net loss to the economy, a loss experienced by white-employing firms and black workers and a lesser gain experienced by black-employing firms and white workers (Becker, 1966). A move that immediately eliminated discrimination in employment would bring a potential gain to all, though it would require some means of compensating those who would directly lose.

A rapid rate of expansion of a country's wealth makes it unnecessary to allow for compensation from the existing social product; it can be made from the natural increase in the social product. As a consequence, a greater possibility of collective action exists when the rate of increase is large.

I have listed two types of current asset held by Negroes, political assets and expanding national wealth which can help to overcome deficits. This list is only a beginning, and any analysis would require the list to be longer and more systematic. Here it is possible to give only an outline of the approach that appears possible and useful. The two assets listed above will serve the purposes of that outline.

PART II

The Conversion of Assets

In gaining some idea of the efficacy of various types of social action and social policy toward erasing the deficits described above, the most important question is the convertibility of assets of one type into assets of another. For example, if the deficits in black freedom of action because of skin color were to be erased, what would be the extent and timing of increased economic resources? The answers to these questions of convertibility of assets are most important for public policy.

I suggest that the general framework within which these interdependencies can be usefully considered is the system of resources implied in the above. A variety of theories of social change is discussed below, each of which in effect hypothesizes certain convertibilities. Many of these hypotheses are in implicit or explicit conflict, and therefore a primary order of business is to gain a better idea of the convertibility of assets in each of these areas to resources in others.

The hypotheses about social change ordinarily focus on particular kinds of resources. Consequently the hypotheses will be examined under the headings of these resources. The resource areas to be examined are those discussed in the preceding section: community, family, personal, legal and legislative, economic, and political.

1. RESOURCES OF BLACK COMMUNITIES

It was indicated earlier that a low level of community cohesion exists in black residential communities. It is useful to spell out in some detail the kind of assets that can be provided by a community and the use that may be made of them.

a. The Level of Interpersonal Trust in a Community

The quantity of trust existing in a community is a resource more directly related to a community's financial capital than is ordinarily realized. I will take a few paragraphs to indicate the intimacy of this connection.

Nearly all economic transactions involve a time difference between the delivery of goods by one party and that by the other. The institution of metallic or commodity money facilitates such transactions by providing a medium that is accepted by one party in lieu of goods. These transactions are even further facilitated if promises to pay, or debts, can be accepted to cover this time discrepancy. In small, close communities, such as the modern financial community in Wall Street, or in some primitive tribes, debts or promises do circulate in much the same way that money does. But in the larger society in which partners to an exchange have no basis of trust for accepting such promises, the government or a central bank itself acts as the debtor and makes the promises, embodied in paper money. Commercial banks make further promises embodied in bank credit. The monetary systems are based on trust, trust of institutions such as the government or a bank,* which makes possible a far greater flow of economic activity than could otherwise occur and constitutes a definite capital asset of the society. In modern society it is usual to conceive of such economically productive systems of trust in terms of the existing monetary system, but in subcommunities of the larger society systems of trust may exist which constitute just as definite an economic capital asset. Two examples will illustrate this. In Lancashire around 1800 manufacturers had little trust in local merchant banks and even less in the central Bank of England, yet they had a great need for money to facilitate economic activity. They developed the use of bills of exchange. These bills or promises to pay circulated from one manufacturer to another as payment for goods received and were guaranteed by each party through whose hands they passed. Had it not been for the existence of widespread mutual trust among these men, economic development could not have taken place with such rapidity (Ashton, 1945).

The second example is the revolving credit associations existing in villages and towns of southeast Asia and Africa (Geertz, 1962). These associations consist of circles of friends and neighbors who, in social gatherings at a member's house, make weekly or monthly contributions to a common fund which is then given to each member in turn in some predetermined order or by lot. Though these systems vary widely, they all take the form of steady contributions and lump-sum payments. Geertz describes the institutions as a means of saving; that is, the accumulation of sufficient

* See Parsons (1963) for an extended discussion.

capital to make a major purchase, such as a bicycle, that otherwise could not be acquired. These associations depend wholly on a system of mutual trust which in effect constitutes a capital asset of the community, for the member who receives his lump sum early must be trusted to continue to contribute if the association is to continue. An extension of such associations was observed recently in Brazil, where a group of men each interested in buying an automobile banded together. All made small monthly payments for a number of months and one received an automobile each month by random drawing. This form of cooperative saving obviously requires a high amount of trust and trustworthiness, both of which are a product of a close, cohesive community.

The revolving credit associations, considered as mutual loan associations, may be compared with the credit facilities in lower-class Negro neighborhoods in the United States. In both cases the persons needing loans have no access to sources of credit at normal rates of interest because their economic positions are marginal. The revolving credit associations are ordinarily initiated by one person who needs a loan for establishing a small enterprise or meeting an emergency. He receives the first payment of the revolving fund. The resulting interest he pays is to his neighbors. The interest remains in the community and is at a lower rate than that offered by the commercial moneylenders. In the absence of the trust on which such associations are based and in the absence of credit from legal lending agencies, lower-class Negroes in America must pay exorbitant rates of interest to a criminally sponsored loan industry. This interest, which is very high, leaves the community and imposes a tax that constitutes a direct economic loss to it.

Revolving credit associations can also be considered as social activities with economic outcomes based on chance, thus bordering on gambling activities. As such, a further contrast may be drawn between the revolving credit association of primitive Asia and Africa and the numbers racket and other gambling schemes of Negro slums in the United States. The result of the latter is a great economic loss to the community instead of a capital gain. In both cases the individual pays a small amount steadily in the prospect of receiving a large lump sum. In the black community, in which the numbers racket is prevalent, the concentration of resources provided by the lump-sum payment is so uncertain that it leads to squandering rather than productive uses. The payments returned are so small compared with the sum invested that the racket constitutes a serious economic drain on the community rather than a capital asset.

Examples similar to the revolving credit associations may be found in many communities. Certain craft workers have developed mutual benevolent societies to ensure one another against the extremities of misfortune.

Among immigrant groups to the United States, as one family became established and economically self-sufficient, it would bring in friends and relatives, helping them until they were established. In Amish communities a man's barn or house is built by a collective community enterprise. In such religious communities, in fact, the principal economic asset is the cohesion of the community, which allows it to confront all problems, internal and external, as a collective body.

In every group with little economic capital such mutual-help arrangements provide as definite a source of capital assets as the more formal money that we ordinarily think of as capital. The point is that although they develop wherever monetary capital is scarce their extent varies widely in different groups, depending on the system of trust that exists in the community. Although they do exist in black communities as a substitute for monetary capital, they often have a meager foundation of trust and are consequently poorly developed. The transiency that characterizes much of the Negro urban North, and in some cases the personal disorganization manifested in delinquency, crime, gambling, drug addiction, and alcoholism, inhibits the development of community institutions based on trust.

The community institutions discussed above have all been direct substitutes for economic capital. Many community institutions, however, based on mutual aid and ultimately on mutual trust, provide assets of other kinds. The collective confrontation of government officials, landlords, or merchants may provide improved living conditions that no individual could bring about. The existence of a community newspaper can conserve the individual's resources by sharing information that he could obtain only with difficulty. The existence of a strong parents' group can exert pressure on the school for results and help it to gain those results. It may be, for example, that among the consequences of the school conflicts in New York one beneficial consequence has been the development of greater community cohesion than has heretofore existed.

All community activities described above depend on an extensive system of mutual trust—a belief in my mind that if I aid you today you will aid me when I am in need—and thus a willingness to make such an investment of resources in one's neighbors.

In addition to the important resources of trust in a community, the nature of the activities themselves can aid or inhibit the sharing of resources. In upper middle-class American communities it is often remarked that resources existing in the community in the form of occupational skills of adult males are wholly unavailable to the children. Sometimes attempts are made to introduce the children to these resources, through a "careers night" or a similar exercise, at the school. On the whole one can say that they are of very little collective use to the community. A friend of an architect's son hardly knows what his friend's father does and is almost never able to benefit from it, to be stimulated by it, or even be informed about the kind of work it entails.

In such communities a set of individual resources that might be a community asset cannot be because of the lack of community cohesion and also because of the particular structure of activities that separates the children from adults other than their own parents. In contrast, in many village communities the social cohesion and appropriate structure of activities exists, so that the children are in contact with adults outside their families. The variety of resources is missing, however, so that they too fail to learn about what an architect does.

This example of sharing of occupational information—or the failure to do so—in upper-middle-class communities shows a case in which the potential community asset is not so directly economic as in the preceding examples. The principle of shared resources holds quite independently of the kind of asset. The important point is that the resource *exists* in some members of the community and that the community social organization be *cohesive* enough to allow its sharing. An important case is that of socialization and discipline of children. Although the family has extensive resources for controlling the actions of its children, they may or may not be shared throughout the community, depending on its cohesion. In a cohesive community a parent need have little concern about his child's activities because he soon learns from neighbors if the child has misbehaved. This may be absent because of the lack of community cohesion—as it tends to be in upper middle-class communities—or it may be absent because of the absence of the basic resource of discipline within the family itself. In many lower-class urban black neighborhoods both essential resources are lacking.

Another important example is the care of children and households in emergencies. In the absence of hired resources, complicated welfare schemes, which seldom function adequately, must be devised to meet the emergencies that occur or else the deficit is transferred to children left to roam in the streets. In every case the community deficit in cohesion becomes converted into deficits—danger, exploitation, absence of attention and concern—that are directly experienced by individuals unless some other asset is substituted in its absence.

In short it appears that the provision of any community asset requires two elements: some set of individual resources that *can* be shared (e.g., the small money incomes of Asian villagers, or the architect's skills in the hypothetical example above) and the cohesion, institutions, and system of trust that allows these resources to serve the whole community. In the United States, middle-class communities have a wide variety of resources but lack the cohesion and trust to allow their utilization by the community. Lower-class black communities lack the cohesion and trust, and except for purely economic resources (which are far more abundant than in a southeast Asian village) lack many of the resources as well. Thus both elements are deficient and both must be supplied if a given community asset is to come into existence. The community cohesion and trust act as a "multiplier," multiplying the assets of individuals by the number of individuals to make the assets of all available to each. For this multiplication to provide a significant asset as a product, both terms must be of some size.

This situation is what economists describe as the free-rider problem. Public services, such as a fire department which serves the whole community, cannot be provided without formal tax enforcement or informal community norms that constrain each person to pay his share. Otherwise all would become "free riders" and the activity would fail. A rotating credit association or a mutual benefit association is like a public service in that each person contributes to it and each receives a return worth more to him than his contribution (a lump-sum payment or insurance against a catastrophe).

The multiplication of individual resources by the size of the community in the case of perfect sharing of resources indicates the interaction that exists between different types of resource. In this case the creation of a capital asset depends on the existence of both the resource of community cohesion and individual resources. More generally community cohesion and trust act as a multiplier of assets and a facilitator of social action. As indicated in the examples, this is an asset that is directly translatable into economic capital or political power.

There appears to be little question about, and little need for, research concerning the multiplier effects of the assets of community trust and cohesion. Yet there are major unsolved questions which research could solve. How is the cohesion and trust created and what are the resources that lead to its development in a community?

2. FAMILY RESOURCES

The importance of the family as the principal socializing agent of the child is well known. What has only recently become evident is the great strength of the family's influence in relation to other socializing agents; for example, several studies comparing the relative importance of variations in family background and school quality on the scholastic achievement of children show the much greater effects of variations in the family [see U.S. Office of Education, 1966, Department of Education and Science (England), 1967, and U.S. Commission on Civil Rights, 1967]. Jackson and Marsden (1964) show the continuity of the family's socializing effects over two or more generations, as reflected in the ability of families displaced from the middle class in one generation to guide their children back to it in the next. More general evidence on the socialization patterns of ethnic groups shows the correlation between the strength of the family and the levels of achievement and delinquency.

As a determinant not only of achievement but of a child's personal resources generally the family appears to have a degree of importance not approached by any other factor.

This is a sword that cuts both ways, for it means not only that the assets of the family will be transmitted to the child but also that its liabilities will become the liabilities of the child. Family resources cannot be supplied or withheld by government policy, as can some others. And it is in family resources that blacks have probably the greatest liability. They are both cultural—the absence of cultural traditions that guide and assist parents in socializing their children—and structural. The structural liabilities consist in the absence of a strong male role in the family and the number of families in which the father is absent entirely or only intermittently present. Moynihan (1965) and others argue, with some evidence, that it is particularly the structural defects that prevent the growth of economic and socialization resources.

This set of conditions creates a difficult situation for social change. The effect of family resources on personal resources is quite clear and evidently quite strong. Lack of family resources, however, appears to be a major liability for lower-class Negroes and one which is at least as difficult to modify as a lack of personal resources themselves.

Such a situation would appear to lead to three possible avenues of change: attempts to increase family resources and thus indirectly the personal resources; attempts to reduce the strength of the family's effect on the child's personal resources, either by greatly increasing the strength of other socializing agents, or reducing the child's contact with the family; and finally provision of external aids, which allow families with a low level of resources nevertheless to socialize their children more effectively. An example of the third is effective community or police action to control delinquent behavior which aids parents otherwise unable to insulate their children from delinquent influences.

Modern totalitarian regimes have faced the problem of breaking the strength of family socialization in the period immediately after taking power. This was done both in Hitler's Germany and in Stalin's Russia by the use of boarding schools and strong youth associations acting as age-specific autosocializing groups. Though it is not a question of breaking a family's socialization power here, it is a question of breaking into a pattern in which one generation's liabilities are carried over into the next. American society has shown little imagination and little application in facing this problem of missing family resources. It appears quite possible that an assessment of alternative socializing mechanisms for children (such as organized peer groups) and ways of increasing the socializing resources of families would provide ideas that could greatly assist the socialization process.

Apart from the effects of families in socializing their children and thus transmitting assets or deficits to the next generation, family resources serve in other ways—in particular, as an alternative or substitute for personal or community resources. A strong family constitutes a kind of social insurance that cushions against reversals of fortune, illness, or any other events that tax or overwhelm the individual's resources. Because resources of a strong family may be concentrated to assist any single member, the family acts, as does the community described in the preceding section, as a multiplier of individual resources, allowing each individual to use his own resources to the limits, secure in the knowledge that the family reserve can help him if necessary. A simple example will give the idea concreteness. A merchant with relatives who can provide him with quick loans if necessary can make immediate commitments on bargain or large-lot purchases, which he could not do if forced to depend on the formal banking system.

Yet family resources can supplement not only personal resources but community resources as well. Many activities may be alternatively carried out by the community or the family, with either substituting for the other: disciplining children, controlling crime and enforcing social norms, sheltering or aiding handicapped or otherwise dependent members, and the variety of other functions that communities and families perform. The family and community differ in size and in strength and permanence of attachment, but their potential functions are similar—except for the child-socializing function, in which the community seldom substitutes for the family.

There are numerous studies that show the effect of various family characteristics in the development of other resources. Only two are discussed here, to illustrate effects on school achievement and on income. The first (U.S. Office of Education, 1966) compares the effects of family background factors with the effects of school factors on achievement, when both are simultaneously considered. In addition, the effects of student body characteristics are included as well. This constitutes probably as close a measure as one can obtain of characteristics of the community as they impinge on a child's achievement. The effective community for a child is largely the community of other children in which he finds himself. This is not always the same as the student body of the school, but it is ordinarily very largely so, since schools in this country are focused around neighborhood and community units. In this examination (Table II–1), which is carried out separately for Negroes and whites in the North and South, the school characteristics were probably better measured than family characteristics, since the former were obtained from information provided by principal, teachers, and students in each school. The latter were obtained merely from students' responses to questions about their families. Thus the relative effects of family background variations is, if anything, understated. In addition, the analyses do not show effects of family background differences between Negroes and whites but only the effects of variations among Negroes and variations among whites, since the two analyses were carried out separately. The results are given in terms of standardized regression coefficients, which can be interpreted as relative magnitudes of effects.

These data show the considerably greater strength of family variations than of school variations in determining student achievement, even though the tests are designed to measure exactly those things the schools are designed to teach. They show as well the importance of the community of other children in which the child finds himself, particularly among Negro students. The combined importance of family and student body resources is far larger than the importance of either school facilities or teacher resources.

A second analysis, referred to earlier (Duncan, 1969), shows the effects of particular attributes of an individual's family background on his income as an adult. The analysis (Table II–2), carried out with white males from a nonfarm background in the civilian labor force, aged 25 to 64 in 1962, shows the effect on income that would be expected if each of the indicated attributes were changed from the level characterizing the average white to that characterizing the average Negro. Each variable shows the additional effects, over and above those that could be accounted for in the variables listed above it. In addition the effect shown for a given attribute depends

Table II–1. Standardized regression coefficients, showing relative effect of variations in family, student body, and school on verbal achievement of 12th grade students[a]

Resources	Negroes		Whites	
	North	South	North	South
Family	.23	.22	.34	.34
Student body	.21	.23	.09	.11
Teachers	.13	.12	.09	.04
School facilities	.13	.07	.10	.07

[a] Source: J. Coleman (1968).

Table II–2. Differences in average income levels for Negroes and whites and the amounts of these income differences attributable to successively changing level of indicated variables[a]

White income	→	Family background	→	Number of siblings	→	Educational level	→	Occupational prestige level	→	Unexplained	→	Negro income
$7070		6130		6060		5540		4170				3280
Decrement		940		70		520		830		1430		

[a] *Source:* O. D. Duncan (1969). Family background is occupation and education of head of family as a child. The amounts accounted for by each variable are after the effects of the variables to the left of it are accounted for. The estimates were obtained by successive regression equations for whites, then substituting in each equation the values of the relevant variables held by average Negroes; for example, the number 940 is obtained by use of a regression equation including only family background, whereas the 70 obtained for number of siblings uses a regression equation that includes family background as well as number of siblings. There is a difference between incomes reported here and those reported in Table I–5 for 1962, especially for Negroes; $3280 here versus $4018 in Table I–5 (and $7070 versus $7112 for whites). The data in this table are individual for males, whereas the data in Table I–5 are for family income. Also, Duncan's data are obtained from a sample survey of a somewhat differently defined population than that of the total population of the United States used in Table I–5.

both on the effect of that attribute and the difference between Negroes and whites in that attribute.

3. PERSONAL RESOURCES

A number of theories of social change give primacy to personal qualities of one type or another. The advocates of this basis of social change include the sociologist Max Weber (1948), the revolutionary Mao Tse-Tung (1963), philosophers Georges Sorel (1925) and Jean-Paul Sartre (1963), and the psychologist David McClelland (1961). All these men share the view that social change is produced by personal qualities by part of the population. I will give a brief account of the various types of theory before discussing research strategy.

a. The Achievement Orientation Theories

One general thesis argues that the personal qualities of hard work, thrift, and orientation to achievement—whether derived from religious values, from family cultural traditions, from explicit training, or from some other source—are essential elements in much of social change. This thesis has gained its greatest psychological sophistication and most intensive study in the work of McClelland. McClelland's thesis is that the "need for achievement" (which is similar to Weber's concept of the "Protestant Ethic") differs widely in different cultures and within a culture and that individuals and societies (seen as aggregates of individuals) with high need for achievement will in fact achieve highly. McClelland has carried out a number of experiments and action programs that appear to confirm that need for achievement can be considered a general personality trait, that it can be induced by training, and that such induced need for achievement does lead to an increase in actual achievements in the real world. The sociological counterpart of such research is that begun by Weber in his linking together of the Protestant emphasis on individualism and individual responsibility for one's fate, with the rise of capitalism in Western society. The "Protestant Ethic" thesis has been subjected to criticism (e.g., Tawney, 1927) and further research effort since Weber's time. The point of greatest question appears not to be the psychological link between the individualism of Protestant sect religion and a strong orientation to achievement but the social and institutional link between such achievement orientation and economic growth.*

* Several sociologists have disagreed with me that Weber's thesis is an individualistic

Besides the general face validity of the argument that those who are achievement oriented will achieve, much evidence indicates that there are personality differences resulting from different family backgrounds, which have a powerful impact on achievement as indicated in the preceding section. A number of research results show that among different ethnic groups those with families that impose the strongest demands on their children and are themselves strongest (in particular, Jews, Chinese, Japanese) show the highest achievement, whereas those with the weakest and least demanding families (Negroes, American Indians) show lowest achievement. Within ethnic groups as well the relation holds: the social and economic level of the family, which is associated with the strength of the family and the strength of demands it makes on its children, accounts for more variation in school achievement and occupation than do any other environmental factors. Altogether the impact of childhood experience within the family on a generalized personality trait of achievement orientation appears to be quite strong.

The psychological constellation leading to high achievement among blacks appears to be somewhat more complex than suggested by the notion of achievement orientation or need. The aspirations toward achievement —particularly educational achievement—held by blacks, both children and adults for their children, appear to be great, even among those whose achievement is low and stationary. This is obviously a psychological oversimplification, for such blacks might well score low on McClelland's n Ach measures. Yet there is a peculiar and ill-understood phenomenon that appears to characterize many blacks, both adults and youths: an unrealistically high, idealized aspiration, relatively unconnected to those actions that ordinarily lead to achievement of a goal.

A personality characteristic related to, but slightly different from, n Ach has appeared in several studies to be a strong determinant of Negro achievement (U.S. Office of Education, 1966, Section 3.26; Hess and Shipman, 1966). This is a sense of "fate control" or of "personal efficacy," a sense that the environment will respond in an orderly fashion to one's actions. Its high relation to achievement, and the lesser relations than are ordinarily supposed between self-esteem and achievement or aspirations and achievement, may offer some hints about the motivational constellation that operates for these children.

---

one, arguing instead that for Weber an institutional force, the growth of protestant religion, is the starting point of change. I certainly agree with this, but for the present examination take as given the existence of the new religion and focus on what I see as Weber's central point, the effect of the religious ideology in transforming personalities and the effect of these transformed personalities in economic growth.

The propositions under discussion here are of three orders. The first is a very straightforward proposition about the effect of personality characteristics ("values" or "motives") on individual achievement. This proposition can be directly studied by psychological research in the laboratory or schools. It appears, as indicated above, that the psychological determinants of achievement may be somewhat different for Negro children than white children in the United States.

A second set of propositions concerns the determinants of the psychological states leading to achievement. The strongest evidence in this area indicates the importance of the family. The effect of other experiences has been studied by McClelland and others, however, and work by Weber and others has shown the importance of religious ideology in shaping these attitudes.

The third proposition concerns the aggregation of individual achievement into societal achievement. The proposition is that significant change in the rate of economic development in a society comes about as a result of increases in, or a higher level of, the relevant personality characteristics. These characteristics are seen as assets that can be converted not only into individual achievement but also into economic development of the society or subsociety. As McClelland states the hypothesis (1961, p. 337), "The shortest way to achieve economic objectives might turn out to be through changing people first."

b. The Revolutionary Transformation Theorists

A second major variety of the thesis that social change derives from personal qualities is of a somewhat different sort and, as will be evident, more sociologically complex. It is the set of hypotheses characterizing "revolutionary" theorists such as Sorel, Sartre, Mao Tse-Tung, and Frantz Fanon.* The hypothesis that all these theorists hold in common, and is most emphasized by Sartre and Sorel, is this: participation in revolutionary action transforms the previously apathetic masses, by giving them a goal and the hope of achieving the goal. The revolutionary action itself, and the rewards of success it brings to hard work, creates men who are no longer bound by traditional customs, inhibited by ascribed authority patterns, and made apathetic by the lack of hope. This psychological transformation,

* Marx is not a theorist of this class because his theory of social change is much closer to economic determinism. Certain of Lenin's writings do emphasize the effect of the revolutionary movement in transforming individual personalities. However, Lenin was far more concerned with the tactics of a revolutionary movement than with a general theory of social change.

according to these authors, is a necessary prerequisite to social and economic transformation. Applied to the case of blacks in the United States, it would state that the real benefit of the civil rights movement is the psychological change it has produced and is producing in those blacks active in it. A more radical application would be that only by engaging in a real revolution will blacks be psychologically transformed in such a way that they can achieve their goals. For these theorists the revolution plays the same role that individualist religion did for Weber or family socialization for McClelland. The psychological mechanism is somewhat different, however, because it predicates psychological change as a result of the individual's own action, not as a result of his social or institutional context. It is an "action-affects-beliefs" hypothesis. The revolutionary action will change the personalities and belief systems of the revolutionaries. This hypothesis, which is stated with different emphasis by Sartre and Sorel, is related to certain social psychological theories that emphasize the effect of action in changing attitudes (see Festinger, 1962). A second element in the hypothesis is identical to that of the achievement-orientation theorists discussed earlier. It states that the changed personalities will then constitute a human capital that can be transformed into economic productivity and social change.

Some of the "revolutionary" theorists include an additional element in their theories, logically unrelated to the hypothesis of a psychological transformation: that the revolutionary ideology should entail a total commitment of the individual to the collectivity. A total submission of the individual will to the collectivity is essential to this theory of social change, so that the collectivity becomes a single-minded instrument of change. This principle implies the abdication of any right of individuals to hold diverse views, either about goals or about means, and the consequent transformation of the revolutionary group into a single force that can be directed at the enemy. The extent of this ideological directive is well illustrated by a recent attack in China on President Liu Shao-chi by the Maoists. Liu had written that "As Communist party members shoulder the unprecedentedly 'great office' of changing the world, it is all the more necessary for them to go through such steeling and self-cultivation in revolutionary struggle." This statement reflects fully the psychological transformation in the revolutionary theorists' work, but it is now apparently seen by the Maoist faction in China as too individualistic. It has been interpreted by the Maoists to mean that one should "suffer a little to gain a lot" and seen as a perversion of Mao's teaching that one must be totally selfless and "be the first to suffer and the last to enjoy." (*The New York Times*, March 3, 1967, p. 8.)

The revolutionary theory of social change constitutes a sharp contrast with the theory of social change which depends on the Protestant Ethic or individualistic achievement. It is a peculiar combination of individual responsibility and collective authority. The two theories begin together in that they imply a transformation in the values or personalities of individuals (the one through religious beliefs or childhood socialization, the other through participation in a revolutionary struggle), and in both theories the transformation includes the belief that one's individual effort can have great effects on one's fate and on the world. The psychological transformation can be an enormous one, because the social structure in which economically depressed populations have often subsisted are feudal and traditional structures with ascribed status, which inculcate a belief in a static order rather than in change and a belief that one could not and should not by his own efforts change his position in life. These conditions in the United States have been most closely approximated in the rural South, which has been the most economically static region and the one closest to a feudal order in its social structure. It is under these conditions that until recently the large majority of blacks in the United States lived.

Viewed in a slightly different way, these theories of social change all are predicated on the imposition on the individual of a powerful and unchallengeable norm to work, to pursue a goal actively. In the theories based on family socialization the norm is internalized by family training. In the theories based on religious ideology the norm is imposed by the religious belief. In the theories based on revolution the norm is imposed by the demands of the revolutionary struggle and enforced by the revolutionary group.

Beyond their common psychological core the achievement theory and the revolutionary theory diverge sharply. The first is wholly individualistic, the second, wholly collective in orientation. The first focuses on the free individual, able to respond to opportunity without regard for obligations or ties to others, able to migrate to cities or to new jobs. The absence of such individualism is often used to account for lack of economic development in primitive societies. Thus, in a discussion of the development of craftmen's guilds in Yoruba, Lloyd (1953, p. 42) says, "The guild laws do much to restrict competition between members; the Yoruba feels that it is immoral to prevent another man from earning a living in the way that he pleases. Finally, tribal social life, with its polygamy, feasts, and costly funerals, does much to prevent capital accumulation. Tribal values thus seem to be primarily responsible for the lack of development within the guilds." This proposition is typical of those that ascribe the absence of social change to values that inhibit the individualistic response to opportunity. The achievement-motive theory emphasizes as well a freedom from constraints by fellow workers to limit work (Max Weber cites in the *Protestant Ethic* the experience of Methodist workers who embraced the new ideology and had their tools broken by fellow workers for working too hard and producing too much).

The revolutionary theory, wholly collective, denies the individual member of the revolutionary effort any freedom of direction. It emphasizes selflessness, the strength in unity, the necessity to "stand together or fall separately," the enormous power that a single-minded collective body exhibits. Thus these two theories share a common element of individual psychology and are diametrically opposed in their social psychological premises.

Another way of looking at the similarities and differences between the achievement and revolutionary theories of social change or approaches to change is to say that they both postulate the disciplined effort of individuals as the essential resource that produces change. For the first the market system, with its possibilities of individual mobility by individual effort, acts as the mechanism to induce this self-discipline and effort. The second depends on collective identity, the existence of a collective enemy to overcome, and the support of an ideology to define that enemy as the source of self-discipline and effort. This second approach to change tends to appear when the market system has broken down for an identifiable group, thus providing the basis for such collective identity. It seems as well to have an inherent instability because of the special conditions necessary to maintain this identity.*

It is true that these two theories have often been applied to different situations of social change. The Protestant Ethic or individual achievement theories have been more often applied to social change within social structures that have been most open, most characterized by a division of labor, and least characterized by a fixed hierarchical order in society. The collective force theories have more often applied to social structures closer to a fixed hierarchical order. Nevertheless, there are large areas of overlap: the collective force thesis has been applied to systems with an advanced division of labor—though its notable successes have been in the hierarchically organized peasant societies. Similarly, the individual-achievement thesis has been applied to the whole range of social systems, though its greatest successes have been in the least hierarchically organized, most open societies.

This partial consistency of theories and social structures is reasonable, but it should not lead to a false sense of closure, for this dialectic, or one directly analogous to it, arises in all phases of Negro action. The problem at a

---

* A very reasonable interpretation of the activities of the Red Guards in China is the attempt by Mao Tse-Tung to recreate the collective identity which was earlier created by the revolution itself.

personal level confronts every middle-class black. Should he strengthen his individualism, discard all past associations, make white friends when he has the opportunity, and let the social change for blacks be the aggregate change due to achievements of himself and others? Or should he bind himself to the black community, a part of a single-minded collectivity, advancing only as it advances? The only ambitious blacks for whom this question does not arise are the leaders in the black movement, for their personal achievements, including sometimes great status and power, are measured only by the collective achievements of blacks as a group. (However, for many of these leaders, the question may well have been raised in the past and their current careers determined by the answers they gave.)

This is the question as it confronts the individual. A modified version of the question confronts the collective movement as well: whether to take collective action leading as quickly as possible to a dismemberment of the collectivity through integration or to take collective action leading to a strengthened collective racial identity and a continued collectivity with increased power. The first strategy characterizes most of the older groups in the civil rights movement and is perhaps best represented by the NAACP. The second strategy characterizes, at the extreme, the Black Muslims and Black Panthers and some youth groups such as SNCC. It should be noted that among all the non-English white national groups in North America it is only the French Canadians whose leaders have often pursued the second strategy, particularly in Quebec. Except for the French Canadians, change has occurred by individual achievement and individual assimilation into the larger society. The same conflict of strategies has beset the labor movement. The ideology of the labor left, principally in Europe, is to maintain class identity and to struggle as a class against the capitalist oppressors. The labor right has taken the strategy of direct economic gains which allow the individual worker a higher living standard.

A similar question confronts the larger society as a collectivity. Which goal on the part of Negroes is most beneficial to the society? Which aim should be facilitated? Individual achievement, destruction of collective identity, and total integration into the society is ordinarily the society's desired goal, for it is such integration that defines the society as an entity.* (The insistence on maintaining a strong collective identity is one reason that Jews have always constituted such a thorn in the flesh to governments.)

---

* It may well be that societies of the future will be able to devise means by which to be more tolerant of deviant minorities within themselves than they have been in the past. If this happens, then the society's integrity need not be threatened by cohesive entities within it that are not subordinate to it.

From the point of view of the most efficient reduction of current deficits among blacks, this question in modified form also arises. The answer is not clear; for example, the increase in collective identity of Negroes which has been partly responsible for the organized movement has been a major asset both in generating other resources and in establishing the conditions for integration. Yet further increase in this collective identity has led to ideologies of separation, of anti-integration, and black racism, which at the extreme constitute serious liabilities.

The answer must therefore be complex, differing according to the type of deficit attacked and the stage in erasing these deficits that has been reached; for example, collective action by civil rights groups appears to have been an extremely powerful asset in reducing the deficit in freedom of social action but a less important asset in increasing economic power.

4. LEGAL AND LEGISLATIVE RESOURCES

Certain theories of social change in the direction of economic development stand at the opposite pole from those theories that give personal qualities the primary place in social change. They can be well exemplified by an analysis that Berle and Means (1932) and Commons (1924, 1950) have used to account for the growth of the modern corporation in the United States. The argument is somewhat as follows. The owners of a company are concerned with the rate of profit on the investment, that is, the rate of return in dividends on the market value of stock. Managers of a company are concerned first with total profit, the difference between expenditures and income, and, beyond that, with expansion of the resources under their control. Thus a corporation in which the policies are closely controlled by the owners will tend to make larger profit yields on capital investment, but smaller total profits, and will be less likely to reinvest profits or borrow for capital expansion than will a corporation in which managers are free from control by the owners.

The joint-stock corporation, with ownership dispersed among many investors, provided an organization in which managers were relatively free from control by owners. In addition, incorporation of such firms is done in the United States by the states, not by the federal government. During the growth of capitalism in the late nineteenth and early twentieth centuries states competed with one another to obtain the incorporation of firms, and since the managers had most control over the place of incorporation they were able to select a state which allowed a corporate structure that would give them most freedom from owners. This freedom included the use of proxy voting, increased discretion by directors in management, the change from unanimous to majority stockholder's votes, the issuance of stock warrants and nonvoting stock, freedom to enter into new kinds of business, and freedom to amend the charter itself by majority vote. The consequence was the existence of a corporation governed by those whose principal aim was growth and whose policies were designed to maximize growth, regardless of its effect in depressing the profit yield on investment.

The most prevalent theory in the area of race relations that does not depend on personal resources is a generalization of the Berle-Means and Commons theory of corporate growth. In the Berle-Means and Commons theory the legal statutes, which themselves derived from a particular political competition among states, were responsible for the structure of control of the corporation and thereby its growth. Generalized, the theory is that social change can be effectively brought about through legal statutes aimed at prohibiting certain actions, enforcing others, or allowing still others. The Supreme Court decision on school desegregation of 1954 and statutes in the Civil Rights Act of 1964 prohibiting discrimination of various sorts are examples of actions guided by this theory. This theoretical position is widely held by lawyers, who see it as the principal mechanism for change. In this theory the arena of social action is the court, and any advocate of social change implements his advocacy by obtaining court rulings. A slightly different theory is held by some legislators, who see the same process, though the principal arena of social action is the legislature and social change is implemented by change in the law.

The Berle-Means and Commons theory of corporate growth assumes that men appropriate to the role will come to occupy it, given the distribution of personalities in society, and that the crucial element is the organizational, or ultimately the legal, structure in creating roles that generate a given motivation. It attributes the rise in capitalism in the United States to the appropriate institutional structure, whereas Weber attributed it to an appropriate psychological structure of individuals.

How is this theory different from the theory behind much civil rights activity: that if the white community's barriers to opportunity for blacks are removed, blacks will seize the opportunity and thus overcome the economic, political, or social deficit? The similarity, of course, lies in the implicit assumption that the principal barrier to social change is the absence of the appropriate institutional or legal structure. In part the difference between the theories is one of numbers. The corporate-growth theories imply that *there exist* at least a few men in society who will pursue the goals relevant to the role. The civil rights theory implies that a *large number* of blacks will be able to fill adequately a new set of roles that is opened up to them. In part the latter theories imply an additional strong condition: that since blacks must compete for these newly opened roles with whites they can effectively do so despite other liabilities. Obviously this is a strong assumption that few persons would make; and it is an assumption not made by the corporate-growth theory.

Thus it is evident that theories which disregard individual personal qualities differ in their assumptions about the supply of implicitly required qualities. Some make only very weak assumptions about this supply, whereas others make very strong ones.

The evidence concerning the direct efficacy of legal or legislative action is mixed. In certain cases legal action has created great social change; for example, the National Labor Relations Act in 1935 changed the terms on which management and labor could legally negotiate, giving legality to certain actions of labor that they had previously not had. The formal power provided by this act did result in more favorable negotiations for unions and was followed by large increases in the size of unions.

On the other hand, the Supreme Court school-desegregation decision had almost no direct effect on school desegregation in states of the deep south. Ten years after the decision fewer than 1% of all Negroes in these states were attending school with whites and in some the percentage was zero. Its only direct effect on desegregation of schools was in border states. It is possible, of course, that this decision will have an ultimate effect by indirect means, one of which is changing the expectations and thus the demands of blacks and sympathetic whites, which would then create the political power necessary for enforcement of the decision. Another is by giving political weapons to parties in other branches of government. The latter means has certainly operated in the case of school desegregation. The Civil Rights Act of 1964 contained, in Title 6, the basis for withholding federal funds from school systems which were not desegregated, a provision that would not have been possible without the Supreme Court decision. It was the use of this economic incentive by the executive branch of the federal government, beginning in 1965, which initiated widespread desegregation in the South.

However, if a legal decision such as the Supreme Court school desegregation decision of 1954 requires an act of Congress and financial incentives in order to be implemented, the importance of the legal action as the source of change is far less than its protagonists allege. It is first of all in part determined by social conditions and, second, depends for its effects on the presence of a variety of additional factors.

Knowledge of the conditions under which a change in the law will have greater or lesser effects is very weak. Certain obvious points can be stated, however. First, if the agent to carry out the action is under direct control of the policy makers, the action will occur; for example, Britain has undergone a currency change to a decimal standard. There was great controversy over the details of the change, but once the law was passed it was certain to be implemented, merely because its implementation lies wholly in the hands of a bureaucracy under government control. As another example, Sweden recently underwent a change from driving on the left side of the road to driving on the right, almost without incident. Again, the implementation of the policy lay within the hands of the government. Similarly, if the school system in the United States were a national one instead of a set of local ones, with each superintendent removable by the national government, the Supreme Court decision would have been implemented immediately. This is easily seen by comparing the school systems on military bases, which are responsible directly to the national government. These schools did desegregate immediately.

Thus a general principle can be stated. *The more nearly a legal action requires implementation by a set of actors who owe no responsibility, direct or indirect, to the lawmakers, the less likely will it be that the action will have an effect.*

Even if we assume a lack of direct responsibility to the lawmakers, a situation may be distinguished in which legal action may be expected to have rather strong and immediate effects. This is the situation in which *implementation of the legal action involves at least one party in whose interest it lies and who is prepared to implement it.* In this case the legislation places a weapon in the hands of one party to a conflict who is prepared to use it. The National Labor Relations Act of 1935 was like this. The law redefined the rules under which collective bargaining could take place, giving more weapons to labor than it previously had. The law was effective because the interested party, labor, was already well enough organized and prepared to take advantage of these new conditions. Similarly, civil rights legislation which allows persons with a discrimination complaint against a place of business to bring the complaint to court can be highly effective when Negroes are prepared to press complaints—but not unless they are so prepared. In a differentiated urban environment social pressure to prevent such complaints can be used only with difficulty, and thus a Negro is free to press a charge. In closely knit rural communities this is seldom so. Also, in some contexts there exists the organizational skill and resources to press the charge effectively. In other contexts there does not. As a consequence the effectiveness of such a law will vary greatly from one locale to another, merely because in one it places a weapon in the hands of the parties prepared to use it, whereas in another no one is prepared to use the new weapon.

An indication of the degree of civil rights organization throughout the

South, and the effectiveness of a legal action when such organization exists, is shown by changes in Negro registration since the Voting Rights Act of 1965. This act, like the Labor Relations Act of 1935, placed a new weapon in the hands of a party prepared to use it, with the result that Negro registration in the South increased dramatically in the years after passage of the act. Table II–3 lists the same data as Table I–9, voter registration in 1964, but includes a column for registration in 1968, three years after the passage of that act.

Comparison of the rapidity of this change as a result of a legal action and the slow pace of school desegregation in the same states suggests the importance of the different structure of action required by the two changes. Voter-registration figures are the aggregate consequence of individual actions of citizens in registering. (To be sure, the transaction involves another party, the voter registration board, whose interests were often opposed to Negro registrants. The effect of the act was to reduce the relative power of this party in the transaction, increasing that of the prospective registrant.) School desegregation, however, cannot be implemented by individual action of the party interested in change but must be implemented by a party, the local school board, whose interests are often opposed to the change.*

Table II–3.   Percentage of voting-age persons who are Negro (1960) and percentage of registered voters who are Negro (1964, 1968) in 11 southern states[a]

	Voting-age persons percent Negro	Registered voters percent Negro (1964)	Registered voters percent Negro (1968)
Alabama	26.2	5.7	19.7
Arkansas	18.5	7.7	16.9
Florida	15.2	7.8	11.7
Georgia	25.4	9.9	18.4
Louisiana	28.5	9.0	21.2
Mississippi	36.0	2.4	26.6
North Carolina	21.5	9.7	16.2
South Carolina	30.6	10.5	23.8
Tennessee	15.0	6.8	13.6
Texas	11.7	5.2	13.2
Virginia	18.9	7.7	16.9
Total	20.0	7.7	16.5

[a] *Source:* James Q. Wilson (1965) p. 956 and Voter Education Project (n.d.).

* This does not explain why the "free-choice" school desegregation plans largely failed to bring about desegregation in the South. More detailed comparison would be necessary to establish the differences between the two cases. My conjecture is that the

Apart from these two principles about the agents of implementation of a legal action, there are certain types of legal action that create an immediate social change. One of the most important involves *situations in which one person loses if he changes alone but no one loses if all change*. This may be termed the "innovator loss" situation. The best example in recent legislation is the law against discrimination in places of business that serve the public, such as restaurants or commercial apartments. Without a law a restaurant owner may not individually desegregate, because if he does he feels that he would stand to lose some of his white customers to other restaurants. If all do, then this will not occur except when attitudes of white customers are very intransigent. The customer knows that Negroes are admitted in all restaurants and thus cannot escape by shifting his patronage. Under such conditions the peculiar paradox may arise, as it has in the recent past in some localities, in which no single businessman would admit Negroes, yet an association made up of the same businessmen favored legislation prohibiting discrimination in their places of business. This paradox can be expected to hold when there is a situation of innovator loss; and when such a paradox arises legislation ordinarily has a quick and permanent effect.

On the other hand, if customers are very prejudiced, there will probably come to exist certain ways around the law: the formation of private restaurant clubs that exclude Negroes from membership, the use of normative constraints by customers determined to keep a place of business all white, and the flight of whites from restaurants in which Negroes have gained a stable foothold, thus encouraging a further increase in Negro patronage.

This example indicates that, even given a particular structure of implementation, the innovator-loss situation in this case, a legal action may or may not have an effect. In this case implementation depends not only on the owners, who face no loss if all integrate, but also on the customers, whose attitudes may be strong enough to lead to countering action.

There is a surprising number of situations in race relations that involve innovator loss. This occurs because much discriminatory behavior arises not directly through prejudice but through fear of a prejudiced reaction on the part of another with whom one wants to maintain good relations. For example, real estate salesmen who show a high amount of discriminatory behavior do so not because of an intrinsically high amount of prejudice but because of a belief that they would lose business from other customers if they did not discriminate. Similarly, a girl may refuse to date a Negro

principal difference lay in the absence of a law that gave the prospective pupil registrant the same power in relation to the school authorities that the Voting Rights Act gave to the prospective voting registrant.

boy not because of prejudice but because she fears that she may lose dates with other boys and be excluded from social occasions by them. The principal difference between these two cases is that the latter is not a situation for legal action, though real estate selling might be; yet in the case of dating, just as in the case of real estate selling, the fear of the reactions of *others* prevents the individual from acting freely in accord with his own desires. In certain cases of this sort the intent of a law may be not to compel but to release individuals from an informally imposed compulsion. Yet the unfortunate character of such situations is that freedom from social compulsion imposed by the prejudice of others can often arise only by an opposing compulsion. Just as the social compulsion does not allow the individual the freedom to act in a nondiscriminatory way, the legal compulsion does not allow the freedom to act in a discriminatory way. If this were not so, such remedies could be applied in many instances in which individual freedom from social constraint is seen as desirable, but not if it is to be immediately subject to legal compulsion in the opposite direction.

These examples suggest the general way in which legal power should be seen. Its effectiveness is not independent of other conditions, but depends greatly on them. Yet this has seldom been recognized. The advocates of legal action assume that it is automatically effective. The opponents assume that "every action produces an equal and opposite action," and that the system will adjust to maintain its equilibrium and prevent any change. The matter is in fact much more complex, and is amenable to careful investigation which can show the conditions under which the assets of legal or legislative power have a high convertibility toward creating resources in other areas.

5. ECONOMIC RESOURCES

Theories of social change as applied to underdeveloped countries sometimes take economic resources as a principal independent variable in social change. In this approach only economic factors are important, and rapid economic growth occurs directly as a consequence of input of economic resources. This assumption is behind the idea of creating economic development through the investment of foreign capital. The general thesis is that underdeveloped countries suffer a deficiency of economic resources with which they can create the means for production. The ideas, of course, are considerably more complex than this simple view, but at this superficial level the evidence is quite mixed. In some countries like Puerto Rico, Mexico, Israel, and the nations of postwar Europe there is strong positive evidence of the effect of external capital in reducing social deficits. In others such as India, Egypt, Ghana, and numerous other countries of Africa, Asia, and South America the evidence is just as strongly negative (see Bauer, 1966, and Ward, 1966). The external capital provided to Western Europe through the Marshall Plan after World War II was highly effective in fostering massive social and economic change. Economic aid with similar purpose in Asia, Africa, and South America has usually been ineffective in producing change, even when accompanied by technical assistance far more extensive than that provided under the Marshall Plan. It seems clear even at this superficial level that the efficacy of economic resources from the outside depends heavily on other factors in the society. There are enough cases of three types to allow a definite conclusion: type (1) cases in which social and economic change occurred even without external economic resources; type (2) cases in which change occurred in the presence of external economic resources, but not without it; and type (3) cases in which change did not occur even in the presence of external economic resources. From these cases it is clear that, for societies as wholes, external economic resources are neither necessary nor sufficient for changes that reduces social deficits, but can aid in bringing about change if "other conditions" are present. This, of course, does not carry matters very far, but it does suggest a simple two-factor conception of change at the most superficial level. A given system of personal, social, and economic organization has the capacity to convert a unit of economic resources into x units of output per unit time.* If there are c units of economic capital, the output per unit time, which determines economic growth, is xc. In some systems the addition of external capital c' will lead to rapid increase in growth because the conversion capacity of the system is great and the capital is low. The countries of Western Europe were in this situation and thus made remarkable gains in only four years of Marshall Plan aid. In other systems it is this conversion capacity itself that is deficient, and the addition of external capital will have little effect on growth. This way of looking at change in a

* If we think of economic production as consisting of a sequence of stages from raw materials to final product and each of these stages requiring a certain mode of industrial organization or productive potential, then x_i is the productive potential of a given stage. The output per unit time is the product of $n + 1$ factors: $x_1 x_2 \ldots x_n c$. This provides a more appropriate sense of the complexity of the problem than a simple product xc of productive potential and capital. It indicates also that even the introduction of technical assistance to increase x_n and x_{n-1} along with capital resources will not affect productivity if productive potential at other stages, x_1 or x_2 is absent. Even more, if an element of productive potential is introduced from outside in the form of technical and organizational skills, without providing a means of subsequently generating it internally, its subsequent withdrawal will leave the country as unproductive as before.

system as a product of economic resources and the system's conversion potential is little more than a formalization of common sense, but it is common sense that has often been missing from foreign aid programs. This does sensitize one to the importance of both elements, and the fact that the absence of growth may be due to the absence of one or the other or both.*

The reduction of deficits of groups within a society through economic resources involves several different kinds of social policy, with different theoretical assumptions underlying them. Three somewhat different sets of assumptions can be identified by rough description of three policies: those that provide *jobs*, those that provide *money*, and those that provide *goods and services*. In the normal economy of the household an outside job brings income that is used to buy goods and services which in turn sustain and improve that labor; that is, productive labor is an asset converted into money that is converted into goods and services which provide the sustenance for further productive labor. In a household that is not economically self-sufficient, additional inputs must be made at one of the three points in this cycle: jobs, money, or goods and services. It is the lack of goods and services that constitute the directly experienced economic deficit for certain households. Different policies, however, have aimed not only at supplying these directly but at providing either jobs or money.

In this chain of resources it is useful to identify several different hypotheses implied by policies that provide inputs at each point. First, however, there must be a division between policies designed to reconstitute a self-sufficient cycle, the household becoming independent of external inputs, and policies designed to provide permanent continued inputs of resources to the cycle. The latter policies envision a permanently dependent set of households supported by public funds. The former envision a final state in which all households are independent of external support.

a. Permanent Dependency

In the case of a permanent dependent population the appropriate policy obviously depends on what resources in this cycle are seen as the ultimate resources satisfying primary needs. Ordinarily they are the goods and services themselves, so that direct provision of those goods and services that constitute the necessities of life automatically overcomes this deficit. Sometimes, however, the primary needs include the autonomy to consume what one wishes, the autonomy to make one's own consumer choice; for example,

---

* For a further discussion of this problem see Barbara Ward (1966) and P. T. Bauer (1966). Bauer goes so far as to argue that foreign governmental aid to underdeveloped countries is almost never of value to the recipient and often harmful.

Dwight MacDonald (1963) argues this in expressing the belief that in an affluent society the standards of support for the poor ought also to be affluent enough to allow expenditures on desired nonessentials. Macdonald's general view appears to be one of accepting permanent dependence of a segment of the population. There are also many government policies that provide direct money inputs to the household with no aim of recreating a self-sufficient economic unit, but with the idea of permanent dependency: aid to dependent children in the United States, family allowances in France, disability payments under Social Security. Proposals such as a negative income tax constitute similar devices.

Finally, productive work and the self-respect it entails is sometimes seen to be an ultimately desirable resource. In this case neither provision of preselected goods and services, nor provision of a direct money income, but only jobs themselves would satisfy the primary needs.

Thus even if one has a conception of a permanently dependent segment of the population as a final state, different beliefs about what constitute primary needs will imply different policies in supplementing the resources of the household economic cycle. Little research on the question of where the input should best occur has been done, for it is difficult to define operationally just what is meant by a primary need. Also, research has often confused the goal of maintaining a dependent population with that of recreating a self-sufficient household. One comparative measure would be the overall level of satisfaction of persons supported in each of these three ways at equal levels of public cost. Another would be the use of childrearing as a kind of litmus-paper test. At the same level of expenditure of public resources which of the sets of families supported in these three ways provide their children with the greatest personal resources with which to enter the larger world? The crucial difference between the criteria here and those under the "self-liquidating support" assumption discussed below is that here the criteria do not include the movement toward self-sufficiency but only the stable level of satisfaction for a given degree of public support. If, for example, goods and services are directly supplied by subsidies to housing, food, and other commodities, does this give the consumer a level of satisfaction as high as the one he would achieve if he made his own choices? If money is directly provided, will it be spent in a way to increase overall satisfaction or to satisfy an artificially created demand and whims of the moment? If jobs are provided, either by a greater demand for labor or by public works outside the labor market, will there be anyone from the most economically deficient households able to hold even a sheltered job? It is these questions, even given the goal of permanent dependence, that must be asked in assessing the relative virtue of various types of economic input in the production-consumption cycle of the household.

Except for several points, we might dismiss this general perspective as envisioning a set of second-class dependent citizens inappropriate to a conception of the good society. One is that in some economies subsidies to workers are designed to support certain industries by allowing direct wages to be low. Housing and food subsidies to those with low incomes, for example, are rather standard partial substitutes for wages in European countries. Such subsidies, used as wage supplements, are not merely support for households but a subsidy to low-wage labor-intensive industries. The cost of the subsidy must then be compared with other forms of income maintenance, for such income supplements may be an alternative to higher levels of unemployment if the noncompetitive industries were forced out of business by higher wages. The question becomes a complicated one for joint study by economists and sociologists to estimate the total cost to the economy of maintaining noncompetitive enterprises and to balance it against an estimate of the costs of permanent maintenance of noncompetitive workers and their households (and any loss in satisfaction due to a permanent dependent status) in an economy in which industry is highly competitive and only highly productive workers are employable. The basic problem is that although noncompetitive or subsidized industries may constitute a drain on the economy which is removed when they are forced out of business, noncompetitive workers and their households constitute a drain that is not removed unless they can be brought to a level of competitive productivity.

To state the matter differently, a society must accept the idea of a set of partially or totally dependent households, either by direct payments or disguised by subsidized noncompetitive industries or public works, unless it is able to train noncompetitive workers to a level of productivity that allows them to be competitive under the given minimum wage standard.

b.   Recreation of Self-sufficiency

Policies designed to reconstitute a self-sufficient household by supplying inputs that will be self-liquidating involve research questions of considerably more interest and complexity. To provide jobs that supply money, money that will buy goods and services, or goods and services that will sustain and improve labor implies assumptions about a point of deficiency in the economic cycle of the household. I will suggest assumptions implicit in each policy and then turn to research results bearing on each set of assumptions.

The economic cycle of the household can be conveniently described in terms of four variables, two on the productive side and two on the consumption side. On the productive side one variable is a general level of productive potential and the second, an opportunity for its employment, labeled x and c for convenience. On the consumption side is first the amount of money and second consumer skill in purchasing those goods and services that will augment productive potential. The money and consumer wisdom are labeled m and w for convenience. Then the normal cycle is one in which the product of x and c generate m, and the product of m and w augments x and also w. If the processes are operating at a level too low for household maintenance, the family is not self-sufficient. In an urban money economy there is a discontinuity in the relation that does not exist in a rural subsistence economy. If the product of potential and opportunity xc is above a given point, the worker holds a job; if it is below, he does not. The hypotheses discussed below involve assumptions about deficits in particular variables.

The system of production and consumption in the household depending on these four factors can be diagrammed as in Figure 1, which shows also the points at which external aid can occur.

The question whether different types of external aid to the family aid in the creation of self-sufficiency is largely whether the aid adds to the capital accounts of the family or only to the current accounts; that is, whether it adds to the family's capability for producing resources or is merely a resource that is used up. Clearly the provision of financial aid, goods and services, and job opportunity adds to the current accounts, and we ask whether (or under what conditions) they add to the capital accounts as well. Aid in the form of job training and consumer education is intended to add to the household's capital accounts. The question is the efficiency with which these forms of aid do in fact provide job training or consumer education.

i. Increasing Job Opportunity Through Increasing the Demand for Labor

This policy assumes in the set of relations above that job opportunity c is the one variable whose low level prevents functioning of the cycle. If this

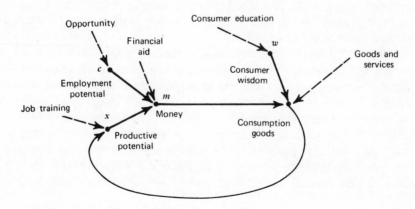

opportunity is increased, all the other variables are sufficiently high to create a self-sustaining household (and by increasing the level of economic demand to maintain high levels of c). In this view the only deficit is a deficit in the employment of resources by the economic system which determines the level of c.

Evidence on this assumption in the United States recently is discussed in detail by Killingsworth (1967). In brief, the results of economic expansion since 1963 (first by a tax cut designed to stimulate demand and increase opportunity, c, and then by high demand created by the Vietnamese war) show that although Negro unemployment decreased, it remained in the same ratio to white unemployment—twice as high. Negro teenage unemployment remained in its same relative position—more than six times overall white unemployment. Unemployment in black ghettoes appears not to have decreased at all but perhaps to have increased. Thus, although increasing c appears to have some effect in reconstituting the cycle of economic self-sufficiency (using continued employment as a rough indicator), its effect appears to be least for those groups that are least self-sufficient, in this case blacks in ghettoes. Given the continued problems of economic deficits of Negroes at high levels of overall economic activity in the United States, it is clear that for many the economic cycle of the household is defective at other points that are not affected by increasing job opportunity.

One body of theory and research regards the level of job opportunity as a determinant of resources quite outside this economic cycle, in particular of stable personal characteristics. This is the thesis that regards delinquency and crime as principally a product of blocked opportunity (Cloward and Ohlin, 1960). In this thesis "blocked opportunity" does not refer solely to economic opportunity, but largely so. Whether in a strong (economic opportunity) or weak (general opportunity) form, the thesis cannot be regarded as well-confirmed. Evidence for and against the thesis occurs in the delinquency literature.

In one recent study of a small group of casually employed Negro men who congregated on the same corner the author himself argues a thesis of blocked opportunity as a source of unproductive lives (Liebow, 1967). His data, however, are not consistent with it, suggesting instead that the whole pattern and orientation of the neighborhood, as well as disabilities in the men's relations to one another and to women, made them unable to work steadily.

A somewhat different thesis is that loss of employment throws an individual into a psychic state that erodes his personal resources. There are many personal case histories of individuals' disorientation and deterioration following loss of a job. One case study of a town in which many of the men were thrown out of work during the depression shows some of these processes at work (Jahoda, Lazarsfeld, and Zeisel, 1960). They can best be summarized as a kind of generalized apathy, a loss of interest in life. Whether this disorientation and apathy constitutes in part a permanent loss of personal resources or a wholly temporary one is not clear. It does appear, however, that an individual's general level of functioning is reduced during the period of job loss.

A corollary to this thesis, that the experience of holding a job will increase personal resources through learning those qualities necessary for productive work, is a relation of similar plausibility but unknown importance. The thesis at its strongest would state that experience in fulltime occupations is the most important element in increasing productive potential.

Examination of work histories, even if these histories contain only minimal information (such as Social Security records), could be valuable in testing this thesis. Such examination would show how the probability of becoming unemployed is affected by such factors as age of entry into fulltime employment, controlling for education and initial income. Obviously, if this effect is a great one, policies designed to increase opportunity, c, would have special benefit, for they act to increase x as well and thus allow self-sustenance even if the level of opportunity reduces.

ii. Increasing Job Opportunity Through Protected Enterprises

An increase in job opportunity, c, through economically protected enterprises (public works or subsidized industry) will obviously maintain the household cycle as long as the subsidy is maintained, for those persons who can hold the sheltered job. If it is to be used to reconstitute economic self-sufficiency, this implies the stronger hypotheses discussed above: that occupational experience increases personal resources enough so that the subsidy is self-liquidating. Conversely, unemployment destroys personal resources. As indicated above, research on these questions would have quite important policy implications.

iii. Direct Inputs of Money to the Family

As indicated earlier, many policies for money supplements to the family are designed as permanent supplements. Even so, if there were effects of these supplements on other resources that would make the household more or less self-sufficient, these supplements could be temporary and self-liquidating. The literature indicates that such ideas are certainly held by some persons. Fleisher, examining statistical correlations, shows a relation between income and family resources and interprets them as effects of income: "A $500 increase in family income will cause a decline in the number of separated or divorced women over 14 by about 2.7 per 1000."

Such statements certainly over interpret the data; but the statistical relationships exist, and research is necessary to determine the directions of cause and effect. (See Fleisher, 1965.)

Some persons go even further than Fleisher; for example, MacDonald (1963) and others argue that a very high level of income support, far above the poverty line, would establish the levels of work motivation and consumer wisdom (i.e., affecting both x and w) necessary for economic self-sufficiency. This is probably nonsense, even if it were economically feasible; but it is very likely possible to test it by careful observation of selected populations who have experienced large windfalls (e.g., American Indians made wealthy by natural resources on their reservations). There does appear to be some evidence against the converse of the thesis: that income loss will destroy motivation and the personal resources necessary for self-sufficiency. The earlier cited study of Jackson and Marsden, for example, found that among 88 working-class children who went into the sixth form of grammar school in England, the last secondary step toward higher education, few were truly working class. Nearly all were from middle-class families who for a generation had suffered reverses and fallen into working-class occupations and income. The economic reverse suffered by these families had left them still far better equipped and motivated to guide their children into academic streams of education than the truly working-class families. From a similar perspective Haggstrom (1964) shows that families with self-sufficient household economies exist at nearly all levels of income and that those with economic dependency are also found over a wide range of income. He suggests that the lack of income can thus hardly be used as an explanation for economic dependency. Certainly it is true that variations in the degree of wisdom in consumption by different households can affect the product $m\ w$ and thus the productive potential just as much as variations in money income.

The possible effects of money inputs to the family are suggested by controversies over the specific way the input is to be made; for example, Moynihan (1965) argues that the payment of aid for dependent children destroys family cohesion because it is conditional on the absence of a male potential wage-earner in the household. It further weakens, Moynihan suggests, the already weak position of the male in the matriarchal family. Alvin Schorr (1967) examines more generally the possible differential effects of different types of money input into the household and is more optimistic about their effects than some of the studies cited above. Obviously it becomes important to learn these effects if the money input is to have effects beyond that of a permanent income supplement.* The question whether

---

* Even if it is conceived as a permanent supplement, it is important to know the ef-

money input will reduce the economic dependency deficit better than job opportunity or goods and services can be answered only if these details of its effects are known.

iv. Inputs of Goods and Services

Goods and services as inputs to overcome deficits of the household economy may cover a wide range. Most apparent are subsidies to housing and food, both of which are more widespread in Europe than in the United States. Also included in this are other services which attempt to affect the productivity of the household directly: education, health services, job training programs, child-care centers, and a variety of community service-agency activities.

As indicated above, some inputs to the household of goods and services are designed only to serve as a permanent external supply of resources, and their value depends on their efficiency in satisfying primary needs. Their merits as resources that help overcome other deficits to produce a self-sufficient household is the point in question here. For this the evidence differs according to the kind of good or service provided. There appears to be considerable evidence now that housing is a resource that has little effect in overcoming other deficits, although plausible arguments for its effects (e.g., see Schorr, 1963) have been given by many authors. Optimistic expectations that "slum clearance" and public housing would reduce crime, delinquency, and other deficits have been completely unfulfilled. Even the effect on health cannot be detected. Wilner, in a carefully controlled study in Baltimore, finds little if any effect of improved housing on health (1962). Glazer summarizes the evidence of the lack of effect of this resource on other social deficits (1960).

Health services would appear to constitute, prima facie, a resource that overcomes other deficits, since persons in ill health frequently cannot be self-sufficient; for example, Brown (1966) examines occupational histories of persons with mental illness and finds a decline in occupational status following first admission to a mental hospital. Fuchs (1966), citing this and other evidence, suggests that the effects of health on productivity and self-sufficiency, over an individual's occupational career, is an important one.

Given this evidence that health resources are important in overcoming or preventing economic deficits, we can go further and ask whether ill health and disease constitute an important deficit for Negroes and for nonself-sufficient households in particular. There seems to be little evidence that this is so, except in extreme situations (e.g., isolated areas in the rural

ficiency with which it satisfies wants under different methods of input. Much of the effort of economists working in this area is directed to this question.

South). Kadushin (1964) reviews a number of studies which show little or no greater likelihood of becoming or staying ill among those at low economic levels than among those at high levels. Rein (1967b), in a study of British medical services, shows that these services are utilized as fully by those at very low economic levels as by those at higher levels.

Thus, despite the fact that health services are—in contrast to housing— a resource that does overcome or prevent economic deficits, there does not appear to be a widespread deficiency in these services which, if rectified, would have a strong indirect effect on economic resources.

There is one broad class of service designed specifically to increase the productive potential of the individual or household. These disparate types of service include public education as a way of making the young self-sufficient and productive, child day-care centers that allow mothers to hold a job, and job-training programs for youth or the unemployed. Little can be said about the efficiency of such services in general for the creation of resources. I will mention only evidence concerning education. A massive U.S. Office of Education survey (1966) shows that in the urban North blacks at the end of high school are in about the same relative position with regard to whites as at the start of the first grade in verbal and mathematical skills. About 85% of the blacks are below the average achievement of whites, about 15% of the blacks (and 50% of whites), above this average. Thus blacks end school with the same relative deficits that their families and neighborhood conditions have imposed on them by age 6. In the rural South the relative deficit increases from 1 to 1.9 standard deviations; only about 5% of the blacks are above the white average.

These statistics make it clear that the system of public education, regarded as a resource that can overcome deficits which arise in the family and community, does not do so for black children on the whole but leaves them with the same or a greater relative deficit in scholastic achievement than the one with which they began. The situation is the opposite to that of health services. Health services are effective in overcoming illness and appear to reduce economic deficits deriving from ill health; but ill health is found little more among low economic groups than high. Educational services appear to be relatively ineffective in overcoming scholastic deficits, and these deficits are quite great for lower-class blacks in relation to middle-class whites.

It is possible to show here how social accounting based on the conversion processes of different resources can be carried out. The example is education, using data from the U.S. Office of Education survey of *Equality of Educational Opportunity*. The convertibility of these resources into achievement in verbal skills was shown earlier in comparison to family resources in Table II–1. However, we can ask a more direct question. What would be the expected achievement of Negroes if each of these clusters of school resources (school facilities, teachers, and student-body characteristics) were increased to the level of whites in the same region of the country or to the level of whites in another region? In order to give some idea of the amount of change this implies, Table II–4 shows the level of resources for northern Negroes, northern whites, southern Negroes, and southern whites for one resource from each of the three clusters. The resource chosen is the one that showed the strongest relation to achievement; however, it must stand as a surrogate for other resources in the same group because within each group the intercorrelations are rather high, thus preventing any statement about effects of specific facilities, specific teachers' characteristics, or specific student environment characteristics.

These differences are not large; however, each of these items constitutes only one of several in the cluster. For teachers' characteristics there are seven specific resources; for the student environment, five; and for facilities and curriculum, eleven. When we ask what the expected level of output achievement would be if the level of input resources for Negroes were equal to those of whites in the same region, the answer is obtained by use of all the resources in the cluster. For each of these resource clusters, and for all three together, the expected achievement of northern Negroes and southern Negroes is shown in Table II–5. In addition, line 6 shows the expected achievement when not only the school resources but also the measured family background resources of the student himself are raised to the level of whites in that region.

This table shows as well a further consequence of the added school re-

Table II–4.   Levels of specific resources for Negro and white grade-12 students in North and South

	Negro North	White North	Negro South	White South
Student environment				
Percentage of student body reporting encyclopedias in home	79	85	62	83
Teacher				
Teacher average Verbal ability (score on 30-item vocabulary test)	22.3	23.1	20.3	23.1
Facilities and curriculum				
Percentage with science lab facilities	93	96	86	89

sources. The Armed Forces Qualifying Test is a test of achievement similar to the one used in the Office of Education study. Before the Vietnam war only men who scored in class IV or above were accepted for service. Assuming that the distribution of scores among these two groups of Negroes would show the same relation to the national distribution in the AFQT as in the tests used in this study, we can estimate the percentage that would be rejected from the Armed Forces on mental disqualification under these various conditions.* These estimates are shown in the second and fourth columns of the table.*

The addition of all three sets of school resources brings the predicted level of northern Negro achievement up four points, a little more than one-third the distance to the national average. Addition of these resources to southern Negroes brings the output resource up five points, about one-third

Table II–5. Expected levels of achievement of northern and southern 12th-grade Negroes when specific resources are raised to level of whites in the same region (national average = 63.5, standard deviation 16.0)[a]

	North		South	
	Average achievement	Percent Fail AFQT Test	Average achievement	Percent Fail AFQT Test
1. Present resources	52.4	20	46.2	33
2. Added school facilities and curricula	52.4	20	46.3	33
3. Added teacher resources	53.9	17	48.7	26
4. Added student environment resources	54.8	16	49.0	26
5. Added all three school resources	56.4	13	51.5	20
6. Added all school *and* family resources	[58.5	10	54.3	15]

[a] *Source:* McPartland and Sprehe (1968).

* One caveat must be added here. The population covered by the survey test is not precisely representative of the age cohort of males. First, it includes girls, and second, it excludes those who have dropped out of high school before the beginning of the 12th grade. Thus the absolute proportions of predicted AFQT failure are somewhat lower than those for the age cohort as a whole, which is 59.6 for Negroes and 14.7 for non-Negroes in 1965, when pre-Vietnam standards were used. However, the predicted changes in those proportions should be unaffected.

* The estimates are made by regressing Negro 12th-grade achievement on measures of family background, facilities and curriculum, teacher, and student environment resources, separately in the North and the South, then substituting in these regression equations the values for those resources held by the average white in the same region, as indicated in the table.

the distance to the national average. In both cases more than half the total expected effect comes from the added student environment resources.

More striking is the effect of these additional resources in reducing the rejection rate from the Armed Forces. Of these cohorts, that is, Negroes who had completed 11 years of school and begun grade 12, 20% of those in the North and 33% of those in the South could expect to fail the AFQT. The addition of the three sets of school resources reduces this number to 13% for those in the North and to 20% for those in the South—again with the principal reduction coming from added student environment resources.

It would be possible, of course, if additional data existed on the relation of these school resources to years of school completed and the relation of achievement levels and years of school completed to occupation and income, to carry this examination of resource-conversion some distance further. Nevertheless, as it stands, it provides the best current estimates of the expected resource output in the form of achievement from specific school inputs. It constitutes for one institutional area the kind of information that is necessary much more generally if those resources currently held by Negroes, as well as those that can come to be employed toward social change for Negroes, are to be used effectively to bring about that change. In this case, although the data are innocuous-looking, they carry a strong policy implication: that school integration will be more effective in reducing Negro achievement deficits than will policies that attempt to give Negro schools those facilities, curricula, and teachers presently enjoyed by whites.

v. Job Training and Consumer Education

The effectiveness of job training and consumer education obviously is specific to the particular program of training. Some social policy has recently been directed toward these ends in manpower retraining, Job Corps and Neighborhood Youth Corps programs. It is likely that little can be said in general about such programs, even when evaluations are complete, because of their variations in goals and means.

There is one experience, military service, that covers a much larger proportion of young men than all the other programs combined. Two questions can be raised about military service: the effects of specified training programs for military service occupations and the general effect of military service in making a man more able to hold a job and perform well on the job. Some research is being carried out on these two questions both in and outside the military. Initial indications are that the answer to the first question is that specific job training is little utilized outside the Armed Forces (Mason, 1970).

Initial results of research directed to the second question show that having military service at the beginning of one's occupational career is beneficial for the jobs one has thereafter and that this benefit is more pronounced for Negroes than for whites. This increment declines, however, over the occupational career so that the beneficial effects of military service are much reduced for the job a man holds 10 years later (see Coleman, Blum, and Sørensen, 1970). It appears likely that military service in general has some definite effects, particularly on rural youth who are exposed for the first time to a wide range of opportunities and demands. In some countries the army has been specifically utilized for the socialization of rural youth into urban life styles. The most explicit use of the army as an educational device has been by Israel, particularly for Eastern Jews.*

vi. Summary of Economic Resource Conversion

Altogether, the question of convertibility of economic resources to other resources for deprived groups within a society is a varied and complex one, with no single answer. In the cycle of economic production and consumption of the home, there appear to be three points at which economic resources can be added and several ways they can be added at each of these points. Their convertibility depends on where and how they are added, as well as on existing resources of the nonself-sufficient households (e.g., their productive potential, their wisdom in consumption, the resources of the family in child socialization). The answers to these questions are precisely those necessary for designing welfare policies that will most efficiently create resources that make the individual and family self-sustaining. Yet the evidence, as well as analogous data from developing countries, suggests that creation of self-sufficiency through economic inputs may have quite limited possibilities in the absence of other changes.

6. POLITICAL RESOURCES

The convertibility of political assets to resources of other kinds depends greatly on the kind of political asset held. The individual vote in an election is different from the organization of votes to support or defeat a candidate, which is still different from organized collective action such as used in the civil rights movement. Perhaps it is most useful to divide the political assets held by Negroes into two classes: (a) assets that are used in formal political processes—the vote in elections, black representatives in legislatures and in other political office; and (b) assets that are used outside the

---

* For an extended account of the use of army experience in Israel as an educational and socializing device see Mordechai Bar-on (1966).

electoral process, usually in direct action which presses demands for change. It is the latter that have been most effectively used by blacks since 1960. Both, however, are important resources and both have increased in recent years. I label the first "electoral politics" and the second "action politics." In the latter I include not only direct action outside legal channels but also those actions that use the courts as a mechanism for effecting change. Both the extralegal direct action and the legal procedures in the courts require the organization and initiation of action. In this both stand in contrast to the act of voting in an election, which is an individual response of an institutionalized nature.

Neither in the case of electoral political nor action political resources will I examine the convertibility of legislative or legal action into resources of other kinds. That question was discussed in Section 4. Instead I will examine the prior step: the convertibility of political resources—political power of either of these two types—into government action.

a. Electoral Resources

The convertibility of the vote into government actions is, of course, not a simple matter because government action depends on the net result of many votes, and blacks are in a small minority in the United States. Yet a number of important points can be stated because that vote has varying power in different situations.

Given a simple majority decision rule in collective choices or, for that matter, any decision rule that requires between 25 and 75% of the vote cast in order to take action, the effective electoral power of a minority group in a democracy depends on its geographic distribution. This is less so in a system of proportional representation in the election of legislatures, for in a system of pure proportional representation the total country is in effect one large constituency. Proportional representation does not exist in most elections in the United States, so that geographic distribution is important in a minority's power. The principal point is that power increases with concentration, for only with concentration will the minority group be in a majority in certain constituencies and able to control the nomination and election of legislators.

In the move from the South to the urban North Negroes have moved toward greater geographical concentration. Even though Negroes have constituted majorities in some counties and even in some congressional districts in the South, they have never been so highly concentrated that whites, aided by disenfranchising techniques, could not outvote them. In the central cities of the North, however, black concentration has reached in some areas the point of absolute control of Congressional districts. In many cities it has reached the point of absolute control of city councilmanic districts, and in some of the largest cities it is now reaching a majority of the total city electorate.

The functioning of the U.S. Congress allows minority group representation, once it reaches the point of electing a representative, a rather high degree of power. A case in point is the power of Adam Clayton Powell, both before and after his unseating in Congress, and his subsequent reelection by his constituency. A parliamentary system with strict party discipline, as in Britain, greatly reduces such minority and constituency power.

The general point, then, is that the convertibility of a minority group's votes into political power that can effect legislation depends, in the American political system, to a great extent on geographical concentration. This can be counted an important defect of a democratic system, for even apart from the techniques used to disenfranchise Negroes in the South it has prevented black demands from being effectively represented in governmental decision-making bodies. However, once reaching legislative bodies, a minority group's interest does have important power in the United States governmental system. These two points together make especially important the projection of demographic and ecological trends for the estimation of future black political power through the vote.*

b. Resources for Action Politics

One of the major changes from the 1950's to the 1960's in Negro resources held is the development of extensive devices for exerting demands on government outside the electoral channels of politics. These have taken numerous forms ranging from court cases to challenge the legality of school districting patterns to actions which violate the law. They include nonviolent and violent action, demonstrations aimed at changing laws regarded as iniquitous, and demonstrations aimed at exercising a legally protected right.

All these actions have the element of collective organization in common and many include mobilization of the populace. One of their effects may be to create personal resources as described earlier, but the explicit aim of most of them is to exert political pressure. The community resources of collective solidarity and trust that were discussed earlier and described as largely missing in black communities have come to exist in the civil rights and black power movements. Thus the enormous multiplication of resources

---

* Useful theoretical analysis of the conditions under which minorities can exert power in a legislature has recently been begun by a number of authors. See particularly Buchanan and Tullock (1962, Chapters 9, 10) and various articles in a young journal, *Public Choice.*

that such collective cohesion provides has come to exist through these movements.

I will not attempt to be comprehensive in a discussion of these forms of political action but will cover only two atttributes: first, the use of nonviolence as a technique and, second, the development of the activities described as "black power."

The principle of nonviolence has been widely used by blacks since 1960. The question I raise is, when can it be a powerful tool; under what conditions is it most powerful in gaining one's ends?

Consider a social conflict in which the lines of cleavage are drawn, with each person on one of two sides. An aggressive action in the conflict will have two kinds of effect on the defender. The first is to destroy, disrupt, and otherwise make ineffective the defender. The second is to unify and intensify the defender's opposition to the aggressor, ordinarily leading to an aggressive response.

Now consider an asymmetric conflict situation, with one side the administrative establishment and the other a conflict group. If the conflict group carries out an aggressive act of civil disobedience, then the administration and behind them the united community, will ordinarily retaliate. The conflict group will in turn be unified by the aggressive response, and respond aggressively in turn, and the battle will be on. However, if the initial act of civil disobedience is not an aggressive one, and if the administration's response is not responded to in turn by aggression but merely by refusal to obey, the second effect of an aggressive action on the administration and general community does not occur; that is, by failing to act aggressively the conflict group does not unify and intensify the actions of its opponent, the administration. *The principal virtue of nonviolence as a strategy is that it does not serve the opponent by unifying his force and intensifying his anger, as does an aggressive or violent act.*

Given this, what does it imply about the conditions under which nonviolence will be a good strategy and the conditions that make it a bad one? The principal implication is that for a monolithic, undivided, fully unified opposition, nonviolence would be a totally ineffective strategy. For an opposition (ordinarily an administrative establishment) that was divided, in a conflict situation in which many persons were uncommitted, and in a situation in which the opposition held humanitarian goals, nonviolence should be maximally effective. Nonviolence depends wholly on separation of the partially committed from the totally committed, and the further pressure of the partially committed on the totally committed to stop the conflict.

Thus several propositions can be derived from this implication. First, the less internally mobilized the enemy, the more effective the nonviolence, and the quicker it will have an effect. Second, the more divergence in strength of commitment between the central core of the enemy and its potential supporters, the more effective the nonviolence. Third, the larger the uncommitted public, and the more influence it can have on the central core, the more effective the nonviolence.

A quite different strategy of action from the strategy of nonviolent resistance is one which has recently developed under the label of black power. The term black power has widely varying definitions, ranging from those that emphasize violence to those that emphasize retail store ownership by blacks. Its essential difference from other aspects of political action, however, is its concentration on the action of blacks in strengthening the resources of blacks. It thus combines the two apparently incongruous aims that have always characterized the Black Muslims: great attention to personal virtues of self-discipline, honesty, effort, achievement; and overcoming the power of whites. It is at one and the same time a self-improvement association and a revolutionary one.

In many respects this direction of the movement can hardly be called political, since it is largely directed to producing personal and social changes within the black community, to self-improvement and self-help. It is political only in the use of these resources for collectively gaining political ends, at the extreme in revolutionary directions. Some of its advocates are explicitly revolutionary, taking their ideology and strategy from the revolutionary theorists discussed earlier, and from very recent writings emerging from the colonial revolutions (e.g., Fanon, 1961). The general strategy can best be described as the use of the power of collective identity to create internal changes in personal resources of Negroes, and to overcome the external enemy. As such it constitutes the concrete realization in the United States of the revolutionary theory of social change discussed earlier.

PART III

Arenas of Action

Although each of the hypotheses or theories of social change discussed in Part II claims a kind of exclusivity as the only or the principal mechanism of change, it appears quite clear that there are a number of different and important mechanisms. Consequently the task of the theorist at this point is not to select which of the theories is correct but rather to set up some kind of framework within which any of the processes discussed above can operate. At the extreme this means nothing more or less than setting up a theory of the social system as a whole. However, it is obviously not possible to accomplish this in one great leap, and the integration to be attempted here is only a first step in that direction.

The integration takes two forms: first, an attempt to discern a few principles or themes that differentiate certain theories from others as a way of summarizing what some of the major differences are; second, ignoring the temptation to select among these principles a set that shows "the" way to change, an attempt to set up a framework for describing more systematically the conversion of resources of all the types discussed above.

One major distinction among theories is the degree to which they interpret social change as resulting from actions of the group in question (either as individuals or collectively) or from the environmental conditions within which members of that group must act (including economic resources, legislative resources, freedom of action, and others). In the first case change is seen as originating from within, in the second, from outside the group in question. This distinction is most fully evident in contrasting the theories described under "personal resources" in Part II with those described under "legal and legislative resources" and "economic resources." Second, within the first of these two classes of theories are those which see the primary actors in the situation as individuals, acting to pursue individual interests, and those which see the primary actors as collectivities, either the community or the political action group.

79

This suggests, then, that these theories see three primary sources of change: the individual member of the group in question, collective actors made up of members of the group in question, and the environmental conditions within which the action takes place. In Table III–1 these are labeled I, C, and E, respectively.

A second major distinction between different theories of change is the different arenas of action within which the processes of change are seen to occur. These arenas of action, such as occupation, family, school, or political collectivities, are evident in the discussion of Part II.

The various arenas of action discussed in Part II are listed in Table III–1, and under these are the theories and hypotheses proposed concerning each, indicating the resources that constitute the primary sources of change and the resources that are, by hypothesis, generated in the change. These resources generated by the process are indicated by the same three symbols, I, C, and E, as for the sources of change. Under each of these is a wide range of resources. Under I are the whole set of personal resources discussed in Parts I and II; under C are cohesion, organization, and trust, at a variety of different levels of collectivity; under E are legal actions, legislative actions, economic resources, and freedom of action.

Table III–1.   Summary of theories of social change

Principal input resource	Description of theory or policy	Section in Part II	Arenas of action	Sources of change	Resultant changes[a]
Community	Community action	1.	Local community	I, C	I, E
Family	Socialization	2.	Family	I, C	I
Personal	Achievement-orientation	3.a	Occupation	I	E
Economic	Job opportunity	5.b.i.,ii	Occupation	E	E
	Welfare (money, goods, services)	5.b.iii	Family	E	I, C
	Education	5.b.iv	School	E	I
	Job training	5.b.v	Occupation	E	I
Legal and legislative	Liberal political theory	6.a	Legislature	C	E
	Legal change	4.	Courts	C, E	E
Political	Populist political theory	6.b	Collective political action	I, C	E
	Revolutionary theory	3.b 6.b	Collective political action	I, C	I, C, E

[a] I = individual; C = collectivity; E = environment.

This table provides a convenient summary of the theories and hypotheses discussed in Part II. The usual practice in sociological theory is to argue or present evidence in favor of one of these, failing to recognize that the social system functions through most or all of these processes. Under different circumstances—different distributions of initial resources—different processes can assume greater importance. It is likely that the tendency among sociologists to focus on one or the other of these is either because one appears important in the particular situation at hand, or else because of a confusion between theory and action in social change. Action involves choosing among these processes in a particular situation, depending on the resources at hand and the desired goals, thus involving a narrowing of focus.* But the theory of change should describe the processes independently of any resources that characterize a concrete situation.

Thus the task becomes one of integrating these various conversion processes into a systematic descriptive framework. Two question naturally arise: the strategic question of how far one should go in the process of integrating these ideas, and the intellectual question of what direction one should go.

In examining the first of these questions, the two extremes are provided by the discussion presented in Part II, left in the form of Table III–1, and at the other extreme a mathematical model together with explicit operations for the measurement of variables entering into it. Toward this latter extreme are certain models of resource transformation in economics, usually described as activity analysis or input-output analysis. I will not go nearly so far as these models go because of the numerous obstacles in the way which would require much more than a short essay to remove; but I will discuss in an appendix some of the characteristics of these economic models in relation to the social transformation processes. The appendix may be regarded as a supplement to this section.

In examining the list of resources and the processes of conversion in Parts I and II, several points become evident that can give some insights about the direction that an integration of ideas can best go. First, it seems clear that one can usefully conceive of a system of resources which acts, through certain processes, to increase or decrease other resources. Second, it appears useful to think of resources acting in a reasonably limited set of arenas of action, with particular actors involved. In economic analysis the

---

* However, more sophisticated action, based on a comprehensive theory, would very likely involve strategies that employed a number of the processes. A comparison with input-output analysis in economics is useful. For a given desired profile of final demand, the appropriate allocation of resources will ordinarily make use of all the industries in the system, except those processes which provide a given resource less efficiently than others in the system.

analogue to these arenas of action is the particular production process, or activity as it is sometimes called, an activity that is conceptually distinct both from the set of resources that serve as inputs and from the set of resources that are outputs.*

These arenas of action may vary from the highly institutionalized, such as the school, to the highly fluid and unstructured, such as political protest. But in each arena it appears reasonable to conceive of several kinds of resource that affect the process. There are resources held by the *actors* in this arena and resources that characterize the *institutional arena* within which the action takes place; for example, in discussing the effectiveness of legal actions designed to bring about greater freedom of action for blacks, such as public accommodation laws, it was pointed out that the increase in actual freedom of action depended on the conjunction of two input resources: the characteristics of the laws themselves, and the presence of active individuals or organizations prepared to make use of it. Neither of these need be considered the primary resource in this situation; it seems rather that the result is a joint product of these two resources.

Interaction between these two kinds of resources can be seen by example. One of these is school desegregation. The school system plans for desegregation approved by the U.S. Office of Education in 1965 were of two types. One was a plan that substituted single districts for dual ones, often in stages to be completed over several years. The second was a "free choice" plan, in which any student could attend any of two or more schools. The second plan worked differentially well in different areas. In the few areas in which it produced substantial integration the reason appeared to be the organized efforts of Negro parents, aided by civil rights groups, to send their children to previously all white schools, in spite of physical and sometimes administrative obstacles. Thus overcoming the deficit of racial isolation in these cases required two resources: first, the political asset at the national level, which led to the requirement for integration imposed by the guidelines, and second, the organized initiative of Negroes in the local community. In those communities where the latter resource was not present the former was not effective.

A second and similar example occurred several years ago in the opening of the building craft unions in New York to widespread admission of Negroes for apprenticeship. Traditionally, apprenticeships had been held rather closely and distributed first to relatives of current union members, thus making it difficult for new ethnic groups to enter one of these craft

---

* In most economic input-output type models the activity is not distinguished from its single product. Only in Von Neumann's general growth model is this distinction made in order to allow joint products from a single industry (see Dorfman, Samuelson, and Solow, 1958).

unions. The political resources of Negroes both locally and nationally, together with the ideological resources found in some liberal union leaders, created enough pressure on the local unions to provide an allocation of a large proportion of apprenticeships for Negro applicants. But there were very few such applicants, with the result that the existing economic deficit was not reduced. The missing assets were the absence of community and family resources that would have generated the organized efforts to produce applicants, and the absence of personal resources of knowledge and motivation that would have led to individual response.

However, this conception of two sets of interacting resources, those characterizing the actors and those characterizing the institutional arena, meets with difficulty, as evidenced by the statement above that individuals *or* organizations must be prepared to act in the situation. More generally, the effect of social organization in augmenting individual resources has been evident throughout Part II. How, then, can it be best introduced into description of the social processes of interest? There appear to be two alternate ways of conceptualizing the role of organizations or collectivities which act as augmenters of individual resources: The first is as actors themselves, as one of the primary components of a social process operating in a given arena of action, with resources consisting of the personal resources of individuals within them and the cohesion, trust, or other attribute of the collective body itself. Alternatively, the individuals themselves may be seen as the primary actors, with the resources of the collectivity acting as multipliers of their personal resources.

A second complication in this schema is that a given arena of action may well involve two or even more sets of actors, with differing resources and with conflicting or reinforcing goals. The outcome of a protest demonstration depends not only the organization and personal resources of the demonstrators, but also on the characteristics of the police and the white community or organization who are actual or potential actors in this arena. In some situations the characteristics of actors other than blacks in the situation can be taken as constant, but this assumption should be clearly recognized.

It is evident that if we attempt to go very far toward formalization of the system at the present, a whole variety of obstacles will arise, even apart from problems of measurement, which we have not discussed. What is useful in this essay is not to open up such a Pandora's box but rather to attempt to create some kind of order from the chaos of theoretical ideas described in Part II.

As a start toward the appropriate integration I will lay out three kinds of relationships in following tables. The first of these (Table III–2) shows the resources that are the inputs for, or affect the level of operation of, each arena of action. Thus this table relates the level of operation of each arena of action to the resources which sustain that level. The next table (Table III–3) shows the resources that are the outputs of, or are produced by, each arena of action. Thus the general conceptual scheme is that the resources held by actors, intensified by resources of social organization and by the opportunities that characterize the institutional arena of action, determine the level of functioning in each arena of action. Each of the arenas of action then produces as outputs resources of different kinds. In both tables some of the resources discussed in Parts I and II are missing, such as the rate of expansion of the economy and the involvement of resourceful whites. A second omission in the tables is any indication of negative "side effects" or reduction of resources of one type by the operation of a given process; for example, the actions of black power organizations have as one consequence the reduction of personal and financial support from whites, and perhaps a reduction in freedom of action as well. Such reduction of resources or creation of liabilities is an omission from the tables that should be recognized in their use.

In Table III–2 it is important to remember that the classes of resource are in some cases quite heterogeneous: "services" include health services, school and child-care programs, and on-the-job training programs, each of which occurs in a different arena of action. Equally, some arenas of action are heterogeneous in the variety of processes or activities that occur within them. In one case, the "family," two processes are separated out; but in the family, as in other arenas of action, there are processes that are not listed separately. An "X" in a cell in Table III–2 indicates that a given resource serves as an input to the process or activity which occurs in a given arena of action.

In Table III–3 the outputs of activities in each arena of action are listed. The table relates arenas of action to the same resources as in Table III–2, but these resources are those either demonstrated or hypothesized to result from the given process. In some cases in which an "X" is listed in the cell the output is well demonstrated to exist; in other cases it is merely claimed or hypothesized but not proved. No attempt is made to distinguish claims from demonstrated fact or strong effects from weak ones.

The final table, Table III–4, gives an indication of what resources appear to interact in affecting the level of operation of activities. Such interaction between two variables means that an increase in either of the variables *intensifies* the effect of the other; for example, the strength of family cohesion intensifies the effect of parental educational background on children's learning. In effect, the result depends on a new variable, which derives from the interaction of the two initial resources. As indicated above, these consist principally of two kinds of interaction: interactions between resources of the actors in a given arena of action and the opportunity or

Table III-2. Input resources to arenas of action

Input resource	Arenas of action									
	Occupation	Family socialization	Family consumption	School	Local community	Elections	Legislature	Courts	Civil rights groups	Black power groups
Personal resources	X	X	X	X	X	X			X	X
Family cohesion		X	X	X					X	
Community cohesion		X			X					
Political movement organization								X	X	X
Jobs	X									
Money			X							
Goods			X							
Services	X	X	X							
Freedom of action	X			X	X	X			X	X
Demographic concentration				X	X	X				
Legal rules, laws					X	X		X	X	X
Political representation							X			

Table III-3. Output resources from arenas of action

Arenas of action		Output Resources										
	Personal re-sources	Family cohe-sion	Com-munity cohe-sion	Political move-ment organi-zation	Jobs	Money	Goods	Ser-vices	Free-dom of action	Demo-graphic concen-tration	Legal rules, laws	Political repre-senta-tion
Occupation	X	X				X						
Family (so-cialization)	X	X										
Family (con-sumption)							X	X				
School	X											
Local Com-munity		X	X	X		X	X	X				
Elections						X	X	X				X
Legislature					X	X	X	X		X	X	
Courts									X	X	X	
Civil rights groups	X		X	X	X			X	X			
Black power groups	X		X	X	X			X				

86

Table III–4. Interactions between resources

Resources	Personal resources	Family cohesion	Community cohesion	Political movement organization	Jobs	Money	Goods	Services	Freedom of action	Demographic concentration	Legal rules, laws	Political representation
												Resources
Personal resources		X		X	X	X		X	X		X	
Family cohesion		X	X		X	X		X				
Community cohesion				X	X	X		X	X		X	
Political movement organization									X	X	X	
Jobs												
Money												
Goods												
Services												
Freedom of action												
Demographic concentration												
Legal rules, laws												X
Political representation												

87

constraints offered by the action context, and interactions that consist of the intensifying or multiplicative effect of social cohesion or organization in its various forms and personal resources. The resources are specified in rather gross categories, so that within each category the specific interactions depend on the action context; for example, an interaction is indicated between "personal resources" and "jobs," which is in fact an interaction between occupational productivity and job opportunity, but since the table is intended principally as a checklist for reference purposes fine detail is omitted.

In Table III–4 an "X" in a cell indicates that resources of the two types specified by the row and column appear to interact, with the result of a joint effect upon the level of operation of the relevant arena of action.

These tables constitute the limits of the integration of ideas from Part II. If the framework is to be useful in any quantitative way for the study of social change, it will be necessary to specify much more precisely the form of the conversion processes, and in conjunction with this to define operationally the measures of resources and the conversion coefficients in each process. It would be fortunate if the precise form of the model could be taken over from input-output analysis in economics. However, the appendix explores this at some length with rather discouraging conclusions. Perhaps the closest to this kind of approach that has been carried out is that described in Part II in two examples shown in Tables II–2 and II–5. These examples involve the development of a causal structure inferred from regression analyses, and then examine how the outputs of the system will vary as input resources vary. In the first example, from Duncan, most of the resources were family-of-origin resources. In the second most were school resources.*

---

* Terry N. Clark has brought to my attention an example of examining the convertibility of input resources in political processes: an examination of differing processes of converting money into votes in political campaigns (Kramer, 1966).

PART IV

Research Implications

If a theory of directed social change is to justify its existence, it must contain within it some point or points at which knowledge can affect action which in turn affects the course of social change. One suspects this is implicit even in those theories that posit deterministic forces of change, but if the theory is to be complete, these points at which knowledge can affect the course of change should be incorporated within the theory and not left outside. Another way of putting this is to say that a theory of directed social change must, to be complete, show how knowledge itself is incorporated into the processes of change. The agents who use the knowledge provided by the theory are themselves part of the system described. Thus the theory should show how such knowledge affects these actors' actions, and thereby the course of change. In the present framework of theory this implies that knowledge, in the hands of particular actors, is itself an input resource for certain processes.

Economists concerned with directed economic change ordinarily leave this element outside their theories—for they implicitly assume that there is someone with power to manipulate the independent variables of their theories. Since theories of social change are concerned with the whole social system including the structure of power in the society, sociologists cannot as justifiably leave outside their theory a specification of how the knowledge it provides enters the system and initiates a chain of action— unless the theories are in fact merely programs for action devised implicitly for the use of someone in a given position of power or with aspiration to power in society.

Consider, for example, one type of theory which at first appears least amenable to directed social change because it focuses on individual personal resources as the locus of change. The theory is that social change is brought about by a high achievement orientation, which in turn is created by certain socialization processes. If the theory is to do more than describe an inexorable fate or be designed for consumption by a person in a particular position of power as a how-to book for his use, it must include propositions about how such information can enter and affect the system, ultimately leading to an increase in achievement motivation.

The first point is to recognize that the research product must itself be located as an element in the system of resources, for in this perspective the research results themselves can constitute resources that, in combination with other resources, help bring about change. This is often implicit in applied research programs, but I suggest it is better made explicit so that the research programs can then be evaluated in terms of the kind and amount of resources they can be expected to produce.

I will not go beyond the first step in locating the research product, or knowledge generally, in the system of action, for to do so would require taking the theory of the system considerably beyond its present point. I simply indicate the points at which the research product, considered as a resource, can enter into the system, and affect the course of change.

The first step in embedding the potential research products in the system of resources is to note that the principal effect of this resource is in modifying the distribution of other resources; that is, the whole aim of this framework of research is to show the connection between inputs to the system and resulting changes. The implicit use for which it is created (besides showing the expected future state of the system under existing resource allocation) is to show how different resource allocations might be expected to lead to different profiles of final desired resources. Thus it is the actions of the actors who have control over various resources that the research product should affect. These actors include different persons in all branches of government and in organizations of the civil rights and black power movements, as well as in private organizations of other types, who control any resources that can be allocated in the various arenas of action described in Part III.

Given this general view of the location of the research product in the system of resources, it is necessary to examine more closely just what research activities will have useful resources that can affect the course of change. One point emerges immediately and that is the overall framework that has been presented: the rather simple idea of viewing the state of the average Negro in American society through a set of accounts that lists levels of resources, together with relative positions of Negroes on those resources that are desired in themselves, and which often show a deficit position relative to other Americans. If this framework, within which processes of social change can be described, is developed with care and imagination, it could have long-range value as a theoretical framework for social change of the types here examined. Its principal present virtue is as the basis for a descriptive set of accounts that can be used for recording changes in the state of Negroes in America and as guides for action.

The first necessary research activity, then, is a wholly descriptive one: to set up a system of accounts, based on careful and frequent observations, showing the resource position of Negroes in America, both as measures of the current conditions characterizing Negroes, in relation to other Americans, and as measures of the resources that can effect change.

In setting up such a system of accounts the headings used in this paper are gross ones; the actual accounts would consist of much more detailed categories; for example, under "personal resources" would come occupational productivity, organizational skills, achievement motivation, educational achievement, and other areas. In addition regional variations, rural-urban variations, and measures of the spread of the distribution as well as the average, are necessary. The degree and type of subgroup disaggregation required remains an open question.

The second necessary research activity is measurement of the conversion factors or transformation coefficients through which certain resources are created from others. Examples that show the beginnings of such research are given in Part II for income and school achievement in Tables II–2 and II–5. This is research of the type that sociologists most often engage in, to learn the effects of certain variables upon others. Yet much more sophistication is required in conceptualization, in research design, and in measurement if the results of the research are to be quantitatively useful in providing measures of the conversion of resources.

A third kind of research activity, which goes beyond the measurement of existing conversion factors, is the measurement of effects of new processes; that is, the existing institutional structure constitutes a kind of current technology within which the system operates in each arena of action. Yet, if certain conversion processes are very inefficient (e.g., if current schools appear to be relatively ineffective in producing achievement in lower-class children), experiments with new techniques may be tried in a given arena. The estimate of conversion factors for these new institutional arrangements or techniques is necessary to show their potential effect on the entire set of resources.

A final research activity is one implied by all that has been stated above: the use of the above research results in a model that will allow forward projection of the system of resources under a variety of assumptions about changes in input resources or setting up new institutional arrangements. Such projections allow the use of these research results in social policy, by showing the expected consequences of various alternative policies. The existence of such a projection model allows the possibility of optimizing:

of specifying the best resource allocation for a desired profile of final resources.

Altogether, the research activities implied by the framework laid down in Parts I, II, and III can probably best be seen by thinking of three kinds of entity: the *level of resources* of various types existing in the system at any point in time, the *mechanisms* through which resources are converted into new resources, and the *arenas of action* within which these mechanisms function. The first research activity is simply a periodic measurement of the state of the resources in the system. The second type of research is measurement of the mechanisms of resource-conversion. The third is measurement of the effects of changes in a given arena of action—changes in the institutional arrangements or techniques which modify the mechanism of conversion. The fourth activity is the use of all this information in giving alternative projections of the system under different resources allocations, and in some arenas of action with new institutional arrangements. I have not described in detail each of these research activities, for each constitutes in itself a research program of some complexity. However, the following sections do indicate a few salient points concerning each of these areas.

1.   A SYSTEM OF ACCOUNTS OVER TIME

The set of resources described in Parts I, II, and III play two roles in the system. Certain of them are the measures of resource deficits held by Negroes in American society. They are the final criteria in terms of which goals or desired changes are stated. At the same time, most or all of the resources are inputs to the social processes through which changes take place.

In their role as current deficits the resources require a *relative* measurement. The measure of deficit is the relative position of Negroes compared to non-Negroes, or of certain subgroups of Negroes compared to other Negroes and non-Negroes. It is this profile of relative positions which is a measure of their effective power over their own lives and over actions of the community and nation.

However, considered as resources that convert into different resources, a measure of the absolute level of the resources is necessary. In this measurement, a fully satisfactory operational definition of the resource is not possible until the form of the conversion process is known. A simple analogy from industrial conversion will indicate how this is so: in the conversion of iron ore into iron the weight of the iron ore is not a sufficient measure of the resource; necessary also is the proportion by weight of iron in the ore. An example in social conversion processes in schools is similar.

As a measure of school resources it is not sufficient to know only the resources provided by the board of education; it is necessary to know the kind of contribution (or at least to have some measure of the amount of contribution) that each makes to the various outputs of the school.

It is necessary, then, to carry out measurement of resources in intimate communication with analysis of the processes themselves, for the processes give appropriate definition to, or descriptions of, the resources that affect their results. This is not to say that measurement of the resources should wait upon analysis of the relevant processes, or be carried out only in conjunction with them. The development of this research tool is a bootstrap operation, and each research activity will be continually refined by the results of complementary activities. It is likely that the measurement of resources should in fact be carried out independently of the analysis of conversion processes because of the different types of research design implied by the goals. One is an extensive estimation of population characteristics and the other an intensive investigation of the conversion process.

2. RESOURCE CONVERSION

The second general type of research complements the system of accounts described above. It is research on the convertibility of resources of one type into resources of another. It is this question, in different terms, to which most of the hypotheses or theories of social change are directed. These hypotheses have been discussed in the earlier sections and will not be reviewed here.

My general perspective here and the perspective I suggest in the design of research in this area is to start by laying out the classes of variables that constitute assets, and to specify the known relations among them. Then the questions that need to be answered by research are specific details about the form of these processes and quantitative estimates of conversion rates, for those that are known, and exploratory information for those that are quite unknown.

The starting point in this research should be the hypotheses described in Part II, and the evidence on which they are based, together with the further discussion of Part III. As is evident, such research constitutes a large program and selectivity is necessary. It is possible, however, to begin by obtaining rough estimates of a large number of the conversion processes rather than by attempting to obtain precise information on a few; for example, census data can be used to obtain a rough estimate of the convertibility of years of schooling into income and the convertibility of freedom of social action by virtue of skin color into income. Some work of this kind has been done, as described in Part II. There are numerous possibilities for further estimates from administrative statistics and census data, and these estimates are crucial for filling out the matrices described in Part III.*

There are several additional points that should be noted in research on resource conversion and these are listed below.

Some of the relationships under investigation have their effect quickly, while others operate only after some delay. Thus it is necessary to design both short- and long-range research; for example, the effect of increased achievements in education on a Negro's economic earning power is an effect that occurs only over a period of time. Similarly, the effect of various school conditions upon achievement in school operates over a period of several years. In both cases fortunate circumstances may make it possible to carry out comparative analysis without examining the same persons over time; but often circumstances are not so fortunate. Thus some research design should include rigorous controls and provision for passage of the necessary time, recognizing that research results based on cross-sectional comparative analysis may often fail to provide conclusive evidence.

A second general point is that any research program must recognize that there are several distinctly different environments in which blacks are concentrated. The urban North and the rural South are the two most important; but there are many Negroes in the urban South as well. A second distinction is between the lower class and the middle class: for the resources of the middle class are different from those of the lower class. Still a third distinction is a generational one. The attitudes of each generation of Negroes are shaped by the events that occurred while they were growing up. Thus the young have political views that are different in many respects from those of their parents, and the consequent composition of political attitudes 20 years hence will be different from that today. Still another important difference is that between an environment that is predominantly black and one that is predominantly white. The actions of any minority group are greatly shaped by its size and demographic concentration, and Negroes are no exception.

A third general point is that studies of resource convertibility are often best carried out as tests of alternative uses of resources for the same purpose, rather than as single separate tests. This arises from the fact that

* Care is necessary in the use of administrative statistics as social indicators, for whenever such statistics are used as the basis for policy decisions by another administrative agency (e.g., a federal agency allocating funds to a locality), that agency will attempt to influence the outcome of these statistics. A simple example is the demand for census recounts by city mayors who would stand to gain federal payments with gain in population.

research methods often do not allow precise quantitative estimates of conversion parameters. Thus results of two studies, each of which examines the use of one type of resource in different arenas and both with the same type of output, will often yield results that cannot be directly compared. Consequently, given the crude state of present measurement, it is often best to test such processes against one another in a single study.

For example, the hypothesis implied by some economists who attribute unemployment to lack of aggregate demand is that a strong demand creates employment opportunities which give jobs to persons "unemployable" in times of weak demand, and these marginal jobs in turn provide training for more highly skilled jobs. Further, in times of high demand employers will train workers on the job, whereas they will not do so in times of weak demand. The hypothesis held by those economists who attribute unemployment to "structural" reasons is that the formal educational system or job training is the principal path of entry into the labor force and that persons untrained in the formal educational system will not be able to recover in the labor force itself nor will job training be provided by employers except in times of extreme scarcity of labor.

The former (aggregate demand) hypothesis implies that the economic costs of creating new occupational skills to a firm, per unit of benefit realized by the firm through those skills, are less than the costs per unit of benefit from alternative methods available—such as use of current workers at overtime rates. Under this condition a firm will hire new workers and train them, thus confirming the first hypothesis.

The second (structural) hypothesis carries two implications: that the cost to a firm per unit of benefit of employing and training new workers is above that of alternative means available to the firm for meeting the increased demand; and that special training programs at public cost will make currently unemployable workers employable at present levels of demand for a cost lower than that of welfare maintenance. Under the first of these implications an employer will not increase his labor force if aggregate demand is increased, thus making aggregate demand ineffective as an instrument of policy; under the second a job-training program will allow these unemployed to be absorbed into jobs.

These competing hypotheses can be tested by careful tests of the implications, by employing resources in alternative ways: artificially increasing the demand in one sector of the economy, thus somewhat reducing the economy's efficiency, a calculable cost per job created; and instituting job training programs, again at a calculable cost per job created. If these hypotheses are to be reasonably well tested against each other, a single design should be used which will result in explicit cost-benefit comparisons of two policy strategies.

A final and more extended point in the discussion of research on conversion of assets concerns the social organization of blacks. It is apparent in much of the preceding discussion that some of the most important existing and potential assets among blacks lie in organization and cohesion. The effect of this organization can be, as indicated earlier, to reduce deficits in freedom of action and political power and to reduce deficits in personal resources. Roughly, it can exert power both to the outside, to change the larger white community, and to the inside, to change Negroes themselves. The organization of the racial movement, the cohesion of black communities, and family cohesion are all quite important. The first, the racial movement, exerts its direct effects on the outside. The family cohesion exerts its direct effects on Negroes themselves. Community cohesion exerts its direct effects in both directions. Because of their present and potential importance in the production of resources, the organization of the racial movement, the black community, and the Negro family demand special research attention.

Most organizations in the racial movement were born as conflict groups. This gives them certain special characteristics: their goals are to win in a social conflict; they tend to be sustained by conflict; leadership of the organization lies with those who are most successful in conflict; and each organization tends to develop particular styles, strategies, and arenas of conflict.

Conflict organizations tend to be shaped and structured by their opposition and by the terms of the dispute. This is most obvious in the effect of polarization upon the nature of leadership. As a dispute becomes polarized, those leaders who urge collaboration and compromise can no longer gain the support of the followers, and radical leaders take over. It is remarkable that in the civil rights movement the polarization process has waxed and waned; it has not moved inexorably forward as is often the case in conflicts. In Little Rock, Arkansas, at the height of the dispute there was no place for moderates, either white or black. The intensity of the conflict destroyed the audience and thus the power of the moderates. Yet since then there have been many subsequent rises and falls in the intensity of the conflict, and in the ability of moderate leaders to gain a following.

It is important to understand far better than we presently do the processes that often carry a conflict into greater and greater intensity, and often push a conflict group into greater and greater radicalism. I say "push" advisedly because the competition for leadership can push leaders into more violent and radical activity than they themselves desire—merely to hold the attention of the followers. It is useful to note that there have been some remarkable Negro leaders in this movement who have managed to maintain their positions of leadership while holding firmly to moderate strategies of conflict—perhaps the best example being Martin Luther King.

The basic point is that a situation of protracted conflict such as has occurred on racial issues in the United States is a very delicately balanced one, which can easily erupt into violence, as has occurred sporadically in this conflict. Yet too little is known about the conditions which upset this balance and the conditions that maintain it. Many black conflict groups have shown great restraint. What are the factors, besides the personalities of particular men, that have allowed this restraint? What changes in the structure of the movement can upset it? An example of the kind of problem to be studied here is the conditions of increasing or decreasing radicalism of conflict groups. Increasing radicalism might be explained by the competition for leadership among different groups in the movement. Certainly such competition exists and its effect is in the direction of increasing radicalism. But why in the direction of increasing radicalism? What determines the direction that such competition leads? And since the radicalism has waxed and waned, and moderation has often prevailed, there are countering factors, some of which may lie in the larger society (e.g., the fact that moderate means have succeeded in gaining legislative action), but some of which may lie within the movement itself.*

For these reasons it is important to have better knowledge of the internal functioning of these conflict groups, and the processes that lead toward and away from violence. The organized movements constitute perhaps the most important current resources by which the deficits of blacks can be overcome. It could perhaps become even a more effective resource for this purpose (e.g., in conjunction with information of the sort discussed in other parts of this research section). It could also run wholly out of control of its leaders, both destroying social institutions and bringing a wave of repression that would wipe out the current assets.

Study of the black neighborhood and community is of a very different sort. The first research task here is merely a descriptive one, to chart the ecology of mutual trust, as well as the kinds of institutions it has spawned —all the way from help between neighbors to investment in a community cooperative. Little is known, in simple descriptive terms, about the pervasiveness of trust and the kinds of community institutions it has spawned. It is evident that this will vary widely from South to North, from rural to urban, from low-density to high-density neighborhoods.

The direct value of trust-based institutions as capital assets in an eco-

---

* For analysis of conflict within social systems and the dynamics of such conflicts see Coleman (1957).

nomic sense is important enough that simply a description of these assets is an important research result. A second research aim should be to discover to what extent a trust basis exists, without as full a development of mutual-aid institutions as the base would allow. Such results would show the opportunities for appropriate social policies to build upon the basis of trust; or conversely, would show what social policies might be expected to fail because of the absence of a sufficient base. A still deeper research aim in this area would be to learn the deterrents to a system of trust, the principal community deficits that undermine the extensive development of a system of trust.

Many blacks are effectively undermined in their attempts at achievement by community disorganization. There would be much support from blacks for efforts to create neighborhood cohesion, but there are many impediments in the way. Since such cohesion could be a valuable asset, it is important to examine in detail the impediments.

There have been many action programs in black communities designed precisely to foster such neighborhood self-help. The combined experiences of these programs should itself be a valuable research result—giving some evidence of what the major impediments are, whether it is in fact feasible to overcome them in all settings, or whether community organization is an asset that can only be achieved as a result of acquiring all the other resources first.

Similar questions can be asked about the Negro family. The effectiveness of strong families is evident in much research; what is not known is how the family can become a strong unit. The "Moynihan hypothesis" is that reconstitution of the role and importance of the male in the family through greater economic opportunity is an important element. Certainly further data beyond those presented by Moynihan can be brought to bear on this question. More generally, what are the principal impediments to the development of a strong Negro family?

Many of the questions posed here about organization at these levels ranging from family to political action group are mere repetitions of what has been said many times before; and certainly there is research in progress on many of them. The most important point of this section, however, is that the results of such research should be seen not as isolated results but as aids for developing organizational resources that are themselves known to be important aids in overcoming other deficits. Many of the questions that arise in governmental action and in actions of the racial movements are questions about allocation of resources: given a limited set of resources, what is their most effective use to generate further resources? It is questions like this for which the results of research on national, community, and family organization are necessary.

3. CHANGES IN CONVERSION PROCESSES

Each arena of action can be conceived as a context within which various conversion processes occur. The family is one such arena in which a wide range of conversion processes take place, the most important being the creation of personal resources in childhood.

In use of the system of resources discussed in the pages above for creating or modifying change two kinds of modifications of the existing system are possible. One is a modification of the distribution of input resources. The simplest example of this is in shifting government appropriations between services such as education or job training, and money income supplements, such as family allowances or a negative income tax. Another example is the shifting of the use of the personal leadership resources from the arena of the local community in community development programs to the civil rights or black power movement.

A second kind of modification of the existing system is one that changes the very processes or mechanism in a given arena. One example is the development of quite new kinds of educational institutions. Another is the institution of the poverty program, which created new mechanisms of change within local communities. A third is the job corps, which constitutes a new mechanism of job training.

This second kind of modification, viewed in the framework of the matrices and vectors of Part III, is a modification not of the vector of resources, but of the matrices of conversion coefficients. This may state the matter too simply and may overstate the difference between the two cases, but the difference is important.* The research required for these changes in process is actual experimentation with the new institutional arrangements: empirical examination of the effects of Head Start, the Job Corps, a new black action group, or a new community-center program. Given the present state of knowledge, it is seldom possible to predict the effects of such processes from the combination of resources that go into them.

Altogether, then, there is one principal point concerning changes in the conversion process. These changes require more than observation of the

* Some equivalences may exist between resources and conversion coefficients. If a mechanism of conversion is complex in form, with multiplicative relationships between resources, then shifts of certain resources may, in one conceptual framework, be equivalent to changes in conversion mechanisms in another. In one conceptual system, the change of a conventional school system to an educational park might be merely a change in the distribution of input resources, while in the other, it would be a change in the mechanism or process itself. Obviously, in either case, it would be necessary to study empirically the effect of this change.

ongoing system; they require experimentation with the changed processes themselves, whether in the form of new organizations or institutions or as new techniques within existing organizations.

4. CONTINGENT PROJECTIONS AND OPTIMIZATION

The fourth major type of research depends on the first and second (and makes use of the third) but goes beyond them. It is the projection of what can be termed "contingent trends," by use of the current and capital accounts of resources, and knowledge about resource conversion. Such projections are simulations of future states, contingent on different actions being taken in the present.

In principle, it is easy to see how such projections or simulations can proceed. If one knows the detailed current state of relevant variables, and the relations between them, then it is in principle possible to project forward that system of variables to show the effect of changes in one on changes in others. In practice, it is more difficult. Although it is frequently done in natural sciences, economics provides the only example in the social sciences. Input-output analysis has been designed for just that purpose and has been used in several economies for modeling the effects of different economic policies. The difficulties that input-output analysis has encountered, although the conversion factors for resources of one type into resources of another are much better known, show the problems that can be expected to arise in making such contingent projections.

The principal rule that must guide work in this area is that action will be taken with or without such explicit projections, and action taken without them will be based on implicit assumptions and implicit mental projections. Thus to be valuable, the explicit contingent projections need not be perfect, but need only be better than the implicit ones otherwise used. Thus they should err on the side of simplicity rather than complexity to provide modest improvements on the implicit mental projections.

There are examples of such projections that can be made on the basis of existing data, and some that have been done. Ecological-demographic projections, for example, show the consequences of current birth rates and residential patterns for the ecology of metropolitan areas some years hence. Another is educational-occupational. Using information about the current structure of the labor force, the rate of change in this structure, current occupational distributions of Negroes and whites, the relation between education and occupation, trends in educational achievement for Negroes and whites, and projected numbers of Negro and white entrants and leavers of the labor force, it would be possible to project the occupational distribution of Negroes and whites into the future.*

Such projections can become contingent projections by the use of alternative assumptions about certain trends. The results would be of the form, "If it were possible to change the educational achievement of Negroes over the next five years in a different way than expected on the basis of extrapolation of past trends, the effect on the occupational distribution fifteen years hence would be. . . ." The education example used in Part II (Table II–5) is an initial start in this direction. They can become optimization models by starting at the other end: by taking as given a desired profile of assets, and asking what distribution of resources will give that profile in the shortest period of time, or a related optimization question.†

Such simulations or projections would obviously require mounting a serious and intensive research effort, using skills and experience from economic input-output analysis as well as sociological skills. The value of the results would be, as in the earlier types of research, to provide the informational base for legal, governmental, and organizational action, as well as to inform the political pressure that can affect such action, in short, to inform those who control particular resources. In particular, projections of this sort can lead groups that find their immediate interest in certain kinds of action, or in the prevention of action, to see that such action or inaction is inimical to their long-range interests.

* See Lieberson and Fuguitt (1967), for an example close to this.
† Richard Stone (1966, 1970) has begun to develop social accounting of this sort which goes some distance beyond that of strictly economic accounts.

APPENDIX

Economic Models for Systems of Resource-transformation

It may be instructive to examine briefly some models for describing the conversion of resources that have been developed in economic theory. These descriptions include both Walrasian general equilibrium theory in classical economics, and modern developments stemming from this. There have been several variations in approach, but all of them will be considered under the general heading of input-output analysis.* Although certain aspects of input-output analysis, such as optimization procedures, may have less relevance here than in economics, the explicit development of this technique as a way of describing the conversion of resources in an economic system holds some attraction. In input-output analysis, the economic system is described by a matrix in which the rows represent industries which supply products both to other industries and to final consumer demand. The columns represent these same industries, now not in the role of suppliers, but in the role of users of the output of other industries. Each entry x_{ij} in such a system of accounts is the number of units of the product of industry i (the row industry) used in producing the output of industry j (the column industry). The sum of these entries along row i gives the total number of units of product i used in all industries, including final demand. It is meaningless to sum down a column because the entries in each row are given in units the product represented by that row. However, column j gives a profile of the relative amounts of different inputs required in industry j. If we divide these entries by the total number of units of j, x_j, which

---

* Some of these approaches are discussed by Leontief (1968), the originator of input-output analysis. Others, including the Von Neumann generalization, can be found in Dorfman, Samuelson, and Solow (1958).

these inputs produced, the resulting numbers a_{ij} are the number of units of resource i necessary to produce one unit of resource j. Their dimension is units i input/unit j output. These numbers constitute a kind of standard profile of inputs for resource j, very much like a cook's recipe or a chemical formula which shows the number of atoms or molecules of each element necessary to create one molecule of the resulting compound.

These coefficients, which are called technological coefficients, represent one of the basic components of input-output analysis. They are assumed, as in a chemical equation or a recipe, to remain fixed in the economic system at hand. The assumptions they imply about the production of resource j are quite strong ones. In particular, if the input resources for producing resource j are in the correct proportions, an addition of more of input i will not affect the output of j; i will merely be in surplus. These technological coefficients look deceptively like linear regression coefficients in which the size of the dependent variable z_j equals $a_i + b_{ij}z_i + \ldots + b_{nj}z_n$. However, they have exactly inverted dimensions (unit of input per unit output, whereas b_{ij} is unit increase in dependent variable j per unit increase in independent variable i). The regression coefficients imply that each independent variable i contributes independently to j, with the resulting size of j being a sum of the contributions of each of the independent variables. This means that instead of a fixed ratio of inputs a totally free ratio of inputs is assumed to be possible in linear regression. If an additional quantity Δz_i, of i were added to the set of inputs, an additional amount of j, $\Delta z_j = b_{ij}\Delta z_i$, would result.

One strong and restrictive assumption of input-output analysis, then, is that resources enter into the production of another resource in fixed proportions. This is appropriate for certain material flows in ecomonic activity. It is hardly appropriate for other inputs to economic production which can enter in varying proportions, such as labor and land in the classic example of agricultural production, nor is it appropriate for many of the social conversion processes under consideration here, in which the creation of one resource may occur through any of several processes, and differing proportions of input resources may be used in any one process. It is, however, where much of the usefulness of input-output analysis in economics lies, for it is clear that if these technological coefficients are fixed, then some complex adjustments must be made to insure that the correct amounts of each ingredient go into each industry in order to arrive at some desired profile of final consumption at a maximum level of production which can be reached. Ordinarily it is the price system through which the system itself solves this problem of allocation; but input-output analysis can be used for exploring indirect effects on prices of changing consumption profiles, and can be used for allocation purposes as a supplement to the price system.

There are, however, some additions and variations in input-output analysis that bring it somewhat closer to an adequate description of the processes under consideration here. Two of these are of particular interest: the introduction of a second kind of input which is not consumed in the production process, and can be considered as capital; and the introduction of an intermediate concept, a set of "activities" which allow the possibility that one activity can have multiple outputs, rather than a single industry producing a single product.

The capital contributions to the production of resources are introduced in much the same way as the flow of materials. For a given technological arrangement it is assumed that beyond the flow of materials represented in the matrix described earlier, each industry requires also a certain profile of capital stocks. This capital consists of products from the various industries, but the amount of product i produced per unit time which goes into capital constitutes an *addition* to the existing supply of capital, rather than merely a replenishing of the flow of consumed resources, as before. The amount of capital resource i required per unit of output j in a given period of time is described by a coefficient similar to the a_{ij}, which can be labeled b_{ij}. The dimensions on b_{ij} are units of capital product i required/(unit of output j/time). The set of a_{ij}'s and b_{ij}'s for a given output j constitute a profile of the amounts of each resource consumed (a_{ij}'s) and each capital resource (b_{ij}'s) necessary to provide one unit output per unit time of j. Any excess of some resource that distorts the profile will simply be wasted or unused inputs.

This modification of input-output analysis brings it only a small step closer to the problem at hand here. It now encompasses both consumed inputs (flows of materials or labor) and nonconsumed inputs (capital equipment). Since many of the resources under discussion in social change are not consumed in the creation of other resources, they are probably most usefully thought of as analogous to the capital portion of input-output analysis. Nevertheless, the same restrictive assumption about a fixed recipe in the production of a given resource remains.

A second modification of the basic framework that brings it considerably closer to the problem of conversion of social resources is the introduction of the intermediate concept of activity by using a framework of ideas developed by Von Neumann in a model of economic growth. Despite definite differences between an economic system of production and a system of social resource production, this model appears much closer than the straight input-output model of the problems of social resources.

It is possible to think of two matrices. One shows the inputs of each resource i into the various activities j, and the second shows the outputs of various products k from each of the activities j. The technological coefficients a'_{ij} of the first matrix are analogous to the previous a_{ij}'s, except that instead of units of product j produced is the level of operation of activity j. The dimension on a'_{ij} is units of i input/unit level of activity j. The second matrix consists of a set of productive coefficients, c_{kj}, which have the dimension, units of k produced/unit level of activity j.

Thus, if we think of each activity in the system operating at level $y_i, \ldots, y_m$, the amount of input i consumed by these activities is $x_i = \sum_{j=i}^{m} a'_{ij} y_j$ and the amount of output k produced by them is $x_k = \sum_{j=i}^{m} c_{kj} y_j$.*

Now this more general model has some extremely useful features from the point of view of economic theory. For example, capital resources, or any resources that are not totally consumed in an activity, need no special treatment. They merely need to be distinguished as a resource, i, with co-efficients of input and output a'_{ij} and c_{ij} such that if depreciation is zero, $c_{ij} = a'_{ij}$, and if depreciation is, say, 1% per time period, $c_{ij} = 0.99 a'_{ij}$. That is, at unit level of operation of process j, a'_{ij} units of this good are required as input, and $0.99 a'_{ij}$ come out as output. In this way resources ranging all the way from those fully consumed in the process of production to those with no depreciation whatsoever can be included.

The necessity for fixed proportions of outputs from a given process appears not as inappropriate for social conversion processes as does the necessity for fixed proportions of resource inputs. For we ordinarily think of a process having a certain rather fixed "set of consequences," despite the fact that the level of operation of the process might arise through varying combinations of input resources; that is, with the modification as described, introducing the intervening concept of activity, with a number of inputs and a number of outputs, the model of the economic system comes some-what closer to that required for the social system.

However, there are a number of important limitations, which probably make even this framework inadequate for the purpose at hand. One is the fact that this model assumes that each resource is a "private good" in the economic sense. Its use in one activity precludes its use in another. For

---

* We can think of the preceding case, with only one product per industry, as a de-generate case of this one, in which there are the same number of activities as indus-tries, $c_{ij} = 0$, except when $k = j$, and the a_{ij} of the single-product case are equal to a'_{jj}/c_{jj} here. There is some conceptical clarity gained by doing so, because the sep-aration of a_{ij} into two coefficients a'_{ij} and c_{ij} allows formation of the concept of level of operation of the activity, as conceptually distinct from the rate of production of its product.

most economic goods this is a reasonable assumption, though even in purely economic activity, there are goods which are "public" in the sense that any number of persons can experience or make use of them simultaneously, without taking from the others. A fire department in a community is a partial public good. Considered as an activity operating at a given level (i.e., a given capacity for putting out fire) for one industry in a town, its resources are equally available to all other industries in the same general area (except for the low probability of simultaneous fires). It is possible, of course, to allocate its costs across activities in some arbitrary way, and then to construct a coefficient a'_{ij} which includes in it a multiplication factor that incorporates the value accruing from other activities' payments, but this is not a satisfactory solution if the number of activities changes; and it is not clear that this solution would be satisfactory even if the number of activities remained the same.*

This limitation would not be serious if it were not the case that many of the social resources discussed in Parts II and III are closer to economic public goods than to private goods; for example, the level of trust in the community, the level of family cohesion, or the demographic concentration of Negroes are not "used up" by any activity that depends upon them, but are quite available for other activities.

It may be objected that these are not resources at all, but are better conceived as components of the "technological coefficient" which is a conversion ratio relating input to output. If this position is taken, it means that the very outputs, such as family cohesion, of the processes under consideration cannot (at least not all) be treated as input resources in subsequent time periods, but instead produce fundamental changes in the system— changes in the values of the coefficients. Thus this avenue leads to some complexity.

---

* If the technological coefficient for the input of this good (i) to activity j is a'_{ij}, that is, a'_{ij} units of it were required for a unit level of operation of the activity j, and each activity were operating at level y, ($j = 1, \ldots, m$), the constraint on this public good i would not be the usual constraint $x_i \geqq \Sigma a'_{ij} y_j$ but rather $x_i \geqq \max (a'_{ij} y_j)$; that is, the units of i necessary per unit time would be determined by the maximum level required by any activity rather than by the sum of that required by all. Even with this, however, the coefficient a'_{ij} which served two purposes for private goods (that of showing the required amount of i for unit level of operation of j, and when multiplied by price times quantity, a measure of the ith cost component for activity j) can no longer do so, since the costs are determined by some allocation of the cost of the maximum required level of i, across the various activities. It is possible that by use of an appropriate c_{ij} this difficulty would be bypassed. If in a given system, with activities operating at given relative levels, activity j required $a'_{ij} y_j$ of i for its operation, but, because of cost sharing, needed to pay only for 0.05 of that much i the costs could be kept straight by setting $c_{ij} = 0.95$.

This approach to the problem of certain intangible resources like community trust is closely related to a more general defect of the economic models for the present use. This is the fact that it is explicitly not the case that each social process or activity requires a fixed recipe of inputs. Nor is the level of the social transformation process determined merely by an additive sum of inputs, as regression coefficients would imply. Further, it appears in many cases that the resources are multiplicative. A man's economic production depends, it seems reasonable to suggest, on the product of his productivity and the level of opportunity. Such product terms have no place in the linear models under consideration. All the multiplicative or other nonlinear aspects of the process are packed into the technological coefficients, which remain fixed. Yet it is clearly the case that some of the most important processes of interest here involve the product of, or at least some form of interaction between, resources that are variables in the system. It seems quite likely that the processes can be best represented by some set of equations that include both additive and multiplicative terms.

If we now try to extract what can be useful from the economic models of resource-transformation, there are the following elements:

1. The idea of a set of input resources, each described by their amount or level in the system at a given time, and each constituting inputs to a process or activity;

2. The idea of a process or activity operating at a given level, which may have multiple inputs and multiple outputs. Although the idea of a fixed recipe of inputs is inappropriate, the idea of fixed proportions of outputs from a given activity or process does appear reasonable.

3. The idea of resources that may be consumed in the process of creation of new resources, as well as those which are not consumed in the process. As treated in the economic models, there are two ways of formally handling this difference. One is Leontief's approach in his dynamic system, in which the basic variables as defined are stocks, and the consumption of these in the creation of further resources is a time-derivative. Capital goods are represented in this system simply as quantities that have a low rate of consumption (i.e., depreciation). A second way is that of Von Neumann, in which each activity has inputs and outputs, with those variables that appear only as inputs constituting the consumed resources, and those that appear both as inputs and as outputs constituting the capital resources.

4. The general idea of optimization subject to a set of initial resource constraints. Although this aspect of input-output analysis has not been discussed here it could constitute, when appropriately adapted to the social model, an important tool in deciding about allocation of resources. For

there is no price system and no competitive mechanism to insure the most efficient allocation of resources for a given set of demands.

I shall not attempt to begin the construction of a formal model describing the system discussed in the text. At the present stage this would serve no useful purpose; but in the very design and execution of research following in these directions it is important to take the next step beyond the present examination into the development of a formal model whose variables can be quantitatively measured and whose conversion coefficients are also well-defined enough to allow measurement.

References

Almond, Gabriel A., and Sidney Verba, *The Civic Culture: Political Attitudes and Democracy in Five Nations* (Princeton, N.J.: Princeton University Press, 1963).

Ashton, T. S., "The Bill of Exchange and Private Banks in Lancashire, 1790–1830," *Economic History Review*, **15**, Nos. 1, 2 (1945); reprinted in *Papers in English Monetary History*, edited by T. S. Ashton and R. S. Sayers (London: Oxford University Press, 1953).

Bar-on, Colonel Mordechai, *Education Processes in the Israel Defence Forces* (Tel Aviv: Israeli Press, December 1966).

Bauer, P. T., "Foreign Aid: An Instrument for Progress?" in *Two Views on Aid to Developing Countries* (London: Institute of Economic Affairs, 1966).

Becker, G. A., *The Economics of Discrimination* (Chicago: University of Chicago Press, 1957).

Berle, A. A., and G. C. Means, *Modern Corporation and Private Property* (New York: Macmillan, 1932).

Blau, Peter M., and Otis Dudley Duncan, *The American Occupational Structure* (New York: Wiley, 1967).

Brown, G. W. et al., *Schizophrenia and Social Care* (London: Oxford University Press, 1966).

Buchanan, J., and G. Tullock, *The Calculus of Consent* (Ann Arbor: University of Michigan Press, 1962).

Clark, Terry N., *Community Structure and Decision-Making* (San Francisco: Chandler, 1968).

Cloward, Richard A., and Lloyd Ohlin, *Delinquency and Opportunity* (New York: The Free Press, 1960).

Coleman, James S., *Community Conflict* (New York: The Free Press of Glencoe, 1957).

——————, "Comment on 'On the Concept of Influence,'" *Public Opinion Quarterly,* **27**, 63–82 (Spring 1963).

——————, "The Evaluation of Equality of Educational Opportunity," mimeographed (Santa Monica, Calif.: Rand Corporation, 1968).

——————, Zahava D. Blum, and Aage B. Sørensen, "Occupational Status Changes for Blacks and Non-Blacks During the First Ten Years of Occupational Experience," (Baltimore, Md.: Center for the Study of Schools, Report 76, August 1970).

Commons, John R., *Legal Foundations of Capitalism* (New York: Macmillan, 1924).

——————, *The Economics of Collective Action* (New York: Macmillan, 1950).

Department of Education and Science (England), *Children and Their Primary Schools* ("Plowden Report"), Vol. 2, Appendix 4. (London: Her Majesty's Stationery Office, 1967).

Dorfman, R., P. Samuelson, and R. Solow, *Linear Programming and Economic Analysis* (New York: McGraw-Hill, 1958).

Duncan, Otis Dudley, "Discrimination Against Negroes," *The Annals of the American Academy of Political and Social Science,* **371**, 85–103 (1967).

——————, "Inheritance by Poverty or Inheritance by Race," forthcoming, (materials for Table II–2 in text are taken from U.S. Dept. of Health, Education, and Welfare, *Toward a Social Report.* (Washington: U.S. Government Printing Office, 1969).

Fanon, Frantz, *The Wretched of the Earth* (London: Penguin Books, 1967; first published as *Les Damnes de la Terre,* 1961).

Festinger, Leon, *A Theory of Cognitive Dissonance* (Evanston: Row Peterson, 1957), reprinted by Stanford University Press, Stanford, 1962.

Fleisher, Benton M., "The Effect of Income on Delinquency," Center for the Study of Social Organization, University of Chicago, 1965.

Fuchs, Victor, "The Contribution of Health Services to the American Economy," (Washington: National Bureau of Economic Research, 1966, mimeographed).

Geertz, Clifford, "The Rotating Credit Association: A 'Middle Rung' in Development," *Economic Development and Cultural Change,* **10**, 241–263 (1962).

Glazer, Nathan, and Davis McEntire, editors, *Studies in Housing and Minority Groups* (Berkeley: University of California Press, 1960).

Haggstrom, Warren, C., "The Power of the Poor," in Frank Riessman et al., Eds., *Mental Health of the Poor* (New York: The Free Press, 1964).

Hess, Robert D., and Virginia C. Shipman, "Maternal Influences upon Early Learning: The Cognitive Environments of Urban Pre-School Children," Chapter 8 in *Early Education,* Robert D. Hess and Roberta M. Bear, Eds. (Chicago: Aldine, 1968).

Jackson, Brian and Dennis Marsden, *Education and the Working Class* (London: Routledge and Kegan Paul, 1962).

Jahoda, Marie, Paul F. Lazarsfeld, and Hans Zeisal, *Die Arbeitslosen von Marienthal* (Verlag fur Demoskopie, Allensbach und Bonn, Satz, Druck und Einband: Druckerei und Verlagsanstalt Konstanz Am Fischmarkt, 1960).

Kadushin, Charles, "Health and Social Class," *New Society,* **14** (December 24, 1964).

Kaldor, N., "Welfare Propositions of Economics and Interpersonal Comparisons of Utility," *Economic Journal,* **49**, 549–552 (1939).

Karpinos, Bernard, "Results of Examination of Youths for Military Service, 1967," Medical Statistics Agency, Office of the Surgeon General, Dept. of the Army (December 1968).

Katz, Irwin and Patricia Gurin, Eds., *Race and the Social Sciences* (New York: Basic Books, 1969).

Killingsworth, Charles C., "Jobs and Income for Negroes," Chapter 5 in *Race and the Social Sciences,* Irwin Katz and Patricia Gurin, Eds., (New York: Basic Books, 1969).

Kramer, Gerald H., "A Decision-Theoretic Analysis of a Problem in Political Campaigning," pp. 137–160 in *Mathematical Applications in Political Science,* Vol. 2, Joseph L. Bernd, Ed. (Dallas: Southern Methodist University Press, 1966).

Leontief, Wassily, "Input-Output Analysis," *International Encyclopedia of the Social Sciences* (New York: Crowell-Collier and Macmillan, 1968).

Lieberson, Stanley, and Glenn V. Fuguitt, "Negro-White Differences in the Absence of Discrimination," *American Journal of Sociology,* **73**, 188–200 (1967).

Liebow, Elliot, *Tally's Corner* (Boston: Little, Brown, 1967).

Lloyd, Peter, "Craft Organization in Yoruba Towns," *Africa,* **23**, 1953, 30–44.

McClelland, David C., *The Achieving Society* (Princeton: Van Nostrand, 1961).

MacDonald, Dwight, "Our Invisible Poor," *The New Yorker* (January 19, 1963).

McPartland, James M., and J. Timothy Sprehe, "Some Hypothetical Experiments on Variations in School Components and Selected Educational Outcomes," (Baltimore, Md.: Center for the Study of Schools, Johns Hopkins University, Report No. 27, October 1968).

Mao Tse-Tung, *The Political Thought of Mao Tse-Tung,* Stuart R. Schram, Ed. (New York: Praeger, 1963).

Mason, William M., The Effects of Military Achievement on the Subsequent Civilian Attainment of Veterans (Chicago: University of Chicago unpublished Ph.D. Dissertation, Summer 1970).

Moynihan, Daniel P., *The Negro Family: The Case for National Action,* Office of Planning and Research, U.S. Department of Labor (Washington: U.S. Government Printing Office, March 1965).

——————————, Personal Communication (June 17, 1969).

Orshansky, Mollie, "Counting the Poor: Another Look at the Poverty Profit," *Social Security Bulletin* (January 1965) 3–29.

Parsons, Talcott, "On the Concept of Influence," *Public Opinion Quarterly,* **27**, (Spring 1963).

Rein, Martin, "Social Science and the Elimination of Poverty," *Journal of the American Institute of Planners,* **33**, 146–163 (1967).

Rein, Martin, Personal Communication, 1967 b.

Report of the National Advisory Commission on Civil Disorders (Washington: U.S. Government Printing Office, 1968).

Sartre, Jean-Paul, *The Problem of Method* (London: Methuen, 1963).

Schorr, Alvin, *Slums and Social Insecurity,* Social Security Administration (Washington: U.S. Government Printing Office, 1963).

——————————, *Poor Kids* (New York: Basic Books, 1967).

Sheatsley, Paul B., "White Attitudes Toward the Negro," *Daedalus,* **95**, 217–238 (1966).

Sheldon, Eleanor B., and Wilbert E. Moore, *Indicators of Social Change* (New York: Russell Sage Foundation, 1968).

Siegel, Paul M., "On the Cost of Being a Negro," *Sociological Inquiry,* **35,** 41–57 (1965).

Sorel, Georges, *Reflections on Violence* (London: Allen and Unwin, 1925).

Stone, Richard, *Mathematics in the Social Sciences and Other Essays* (London: Chapman and Hall, 1966).

——————, *Mathematical Models of the Economy and Other Essays* (London: Chapman and Hall, 1970).

Taeuber, Karl E., and Alma F. Taeuber, *Negroes in Cities* (Chicago: Aldine, 1965).

——————, "The Effect of Income Redistribution on Racial Residential Segregation," *Urban Affairs Quarterly* (September 1968).

Tawney, R. H., *Religion and the Rise of Capitalism* (London: Murray, 1927).

Toward a Social Report, U.S. Department of Health, Education, and Welfare (Washington: U.S. Government Printing Office, 1969).

U.S. Commission on Civil Rights, *Racial Isolation in the Public Schools,* Vol. 2, Appendix C3 (Washington: U.S. Government Printing Office, 1967).

U.S. Department of Health, Education and Welfare, *National Center for Health Statistics,* Series 21, Number 19, "Natality Statistics Analysis, United States, 1965–1967," p. 29 (Washington: U.S. Government Printing Office, May 1970) (a).

U.S. Department of Health, Education, and Welfare, *Monthly Vital Statistics Report,* Vol. 18, No. 11, "Advance Report, Final Natality Statistics, 1968" p. 3 (Washington: U.S. Dept. of Health, Education and Welfare, Public Health Service, Health Services and Mental Health Administration, January 30, 1970) (b).

U.S. Department of Labor, *The Negroes in the United States: Their Economic and Social Situation* (Washington: U.S. Government Printing Office, 1966).

U.S. Office of Education, *Equality of Educational Opportunity,* Chapter 3 (Washington: U.S. Government Printing Office, 1966).

Voter Education Project, "Voter Registration in the South, Summer, 1968" (Atlanta, Georgia: Southern Regional Council, n.d.).

Ward, Barbara, "The Decade of Development—A Study in Frustration?," in *Two Views on Aid to Developing Countries* (London: Institute of Economic Affairs, 1966).

Weber, Max, *The Protestant Ethic and the Spirit of Capitalism* (London: Allen and Unwin, 1948).

Wilner, Daniel, et al., *The Housing Environment and Family Life* (Baltimore: Johns Hopkins Press, 1962).

Wilson, James Q., "The Negro in Politics," *Daedalus,* **94,** 949–973 (1965).

Author Index

Subject Index

DATE DUE

I٧/١			
NO 21 '78			
GAYLORD			PRINTED IN U.S.A.